ICELAND

Jonathan Wilcox & Zawiah Abdul Latif

 Marshall Cavendish
Benchmark
New York

PICTURE CREDITS
Cover photo: © Catherine Karnow / CORBIS
alt.TYPE / Reuters: 32, 105 • ANA Images: 5, 6, 47, 50, 55, 96 • Björn Rúriksson / Geoscan: 4, 22, 23, 37, 43, 44, 67, 72, 79, 86, 88, 93, 94, 100, 110, 128 • Camera Press: 11, 20, 82 • David Simson: 12, 19, 26, 58, 61, 76, 78, 91, 111, 118, 122, 123, 124 • Focus Team: 15, 75 • Geoscan / Jón Kr. Fridgeirsson: 28 • Houserstock: 9, 18, 36, 46, 48, 49, 51, 56, 63, 80 • Hulton Deutsch: 27, 83, 103 • Mats Icelandic Photo & Press Service: 25, 29, 92, 99, 102, 104, 115, 120, 129 • Morgunbladid: 74 • Morgunbladid / Arni Saeberg: 62, 68, 81, 112 • Morgunbladid / Bjarni Eriksson: 40 • Morgunbladid / Kristinn Ingvarsson: 69, 116 • Morgunbladid / Porkell Porkelsson: 39, 107, 121 • Morgunbladid / Ragnar Axelsson: 24, 42, 57 • Morgunbladid / Runar Por: 13 • Morgunbladid / Sverrir Vilhelmsson: 119 • National Museum of Iceland / Ívar Brynjulfsson: 95 • Páll Stefansson: 3, 10, 21, 34, 45, 59, 77, 97, 106, 125, 127 • Photolibrary: 16 • R Ian Lloyd: 1, 33, 52, 64, 108, 113, 117 • Stockfood: 131 • Superstock: 30, 114, 130 • The Hutchison Library: 8, 31, 35, 71, 73, 84, 109 • The Image Bank: 7 • Thorsten Henn Images: 38, 65, 90, 135

PRECEDING PAGE
A girl and her dog playing on the plains at the outskirts of Reykjavík.

Editorial Director (U.S.): Michelle Bisson
Editors: Deborah Grahame, Mabelle Yeo, Crystal Ouyang
Copyreader: Deborah Federhen
Designers: Jailani Basari, Cynthia Ng
Cover picture researcher: Connie Gardner
Picture researchers: Thomas Khoo, Joshua Ang

Marshall Cavendish Benchmark
99 White Plains Road
Tarrytown, NY 10591
Web site: www.marshallcavendish.us

Originated and designed by Times Editions
An imprint of Marshall Cavendish International (Asia) Private Limited
A member of Times Publishing Limited

All Internet sites were correct and accurate at the time of printing. All monetary figures in this publication are in U.S. dollars.

Library of Congress Cataloging-in-Publication Data
Wilcox, Jonathan, 1960–
    Iceland / by Jonathan Wilcox and Zawiah Abdul Latif. — 2nd ed.
       p. cm. — (Cultures of the world)
    Includes bibliographical references and index.
       ISBN-13: 978-0-7614-2074-3
       ISBN-10: 0-7614-2074-6
    1. Iceland—Juvenile literature. I. Latif, Zawiah Abdul. II. Title. III. Series. Cultures of the world (2nd ed.)
    DL305.W55 2007
    949.12—dc22   2006047548

Printed in China

9 8 7 6 5 4 3 2 1

CONTENTS

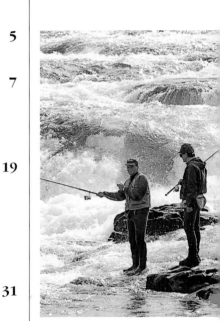

Fishing is a popular leisure activity that is also important to Iceland's economy.

An Icelandic child playing near the sea.

INTRODUCTION

ICELAND IS AN ISLAND of fire and ice. One third of the country is covered by ice, yet volcanic activity creates an abundance of natural hot springs and geysers. Although Iceland is geographically isolated and has less than 1 percent arable land, it has emerged in a single generation as one of the more technologically and socially advanced nations in the world.

One of the world's youngest nations, Iceland was first settled in the Viking age by adventurous Viking settlers. The early settlers organized themselves into a commonwealth governed by the first parliament in Northern Europe. Economically, a large part of Iceland's wealth is dependent on fishing and fish processing. Steady progress has been made in the export of Iceland's other natural resources—geothermal and hydroelectrical energy.

Present-day Iceland is fiercely independent and nationalistic. Icelanders have fought to keep what is central to their identity—their language, customs, and heritage—while keeping pace with the rest of the world. Iceland's current high standards of living and learning are a testament to its success in recognizing the island's potential.

GEOGRAPHY

ICELAND IS AN ISLAND in the North Atlantic midway between America and continental Europe. It is situated just south of the Arctic Circle on the same latitude as Fairbanks, Alaska, but is warmed by the flow of the Gulf Stream. The island covers an area that measures approximately 39,768 square miles (102,999 square km), about the size of Ohio.

Much of the island is uninhabitable. Most of the interior is covered by permanent ice or lava, or is high plateau on which little grows. Human settlement is limited to the rim of the island, where fields have been carved out of the land at the foot of the mountains and where fishing communities have access to the sea. The total population is only a little more than a quarter of a million people, about the size of Akron, Ohio.

Mountainous and geologically active with much volcanic activity, Iceland is full of hot springs and rivers, which often flow down spectacular waterfalls on their way to the sea. The harsh terrain and sparse population have left Iceland a country of breathtaking unspoiled natural beauty.

Left: **This view of Jökulsarion Lake in the winter epitomizes the stark natural beauty of Iceland.**

Opposite: **One of Iceland's most famous geysers, Great Geyser used to spout water regularly to a height of 200 feet (61 m) but is now largely dormant. (The word** *geyser* **is itself a borrowing from Icelandic into English.)**

REGIONS

The most important division in Iceland is between inhabited and uninhabited land. The uninhabited land is primarily in the interior. Half of this is desert plateau above 1,500 feet (457 m), where little grows. Eleven percent of the country is covered with glaciers. Iceland's largest glacier, Vatnajökull, is the largest ice cap in Europe. It covers 3,240 square miles (8,392 square km), almost half the area of New Jersey. At some places the ice of this glacier is over 3,000 feet (914 m) thick.

Inhabited Iceland is essentially the perimeter of the island. This is served by a single highway that circles the island.

One of Iceland's most spectacular waterfalls is called Gullfoss (which means "golden fall"). It is formed where the vast Hvítá River (meaning "white river"), found in the southwest region, falls 105 feet (32 m) into a 1.5-mile- (2.4-km-) wide ravine.

THE SOUTHWEST REGION Over half of the population lives in a small part of the southwest, centering on Reykjavík. Extending southwest from Reykjavík is a peninsula of inhospitable lava exposed to the North Atlantic on which is located the U.S. Marine airbase of Keflavík and the international airport. Farther south and east of Reykjavík is the best farmland in Iceland. Situated inland is the largest lake, Thingvallavatn, covering 32 square miles (83 square km). On its shore is Thingvellir, the site of the first Icelandic parliament. Also found here are the geysers at Geysir.

THE SOUTH Off the south coast are the Westmann Islands, harsh volcanic islands that include Surtsey, newly formed by a volcanic eruption in 1963. On the mainland in the southeast, the glacier Vatnajökull extends almost to the sea. Along the southern coast are numerous *sandur* (SAND-or),

wastelands of black sand and volcanic debris deposited by the glacial run-offs, along with innumerable rivers.

A field of lava surrounds the village of Reykjahlio to the north of Lake Myvatn.

THE NORTH Iceland's second-largest city, Akureyri, is at the head of a fjord in the north center of the island. East of here is Myvatn, also known as Midge Lake, in a fertile valley close to fields of lava. Grímsey, a small island off the north coast, is the only part of Iceland to extend into the Arctic Circle.

THE WESTERN FJORDS The northwest is marked by deep fjords and steep mountains and is inhabited almost wholly by fishing communities. One entire peninsula, Hornstrandir, has experienced depopulation since the first half of the 20th century. Since the area is rich in bird life nesting on the cliffs, it has been designated a nature reserve.

Iceland is a geologically active region, containing about 200 volcanoes. This photo shows a minor eruption in February 1991 of Mount Hekla, an active volcano in the southern interior.

VOLCANIC ACTIVITY

Iceland is situated at the point where two tectonic plates, vast land masses that float on the Earth's central magma, are parting. The plate supporting North America is pulling away from that supporting Europe and Africa. The movement of the plates results in earthquakes and volcanic eruptions. The gap is filled with lava. As a result, Iceland is growing by up to an inch a year.

In the last few centuries, Iceland has experienced an average of one volcanic eruption every five years. The most spectacular eruption in the 20th century took place in the Westmann Islands. Between November 1963 and June 1967, a volcano erupted on the sea bottom. This gave birth to a new island, Surtsey, made of lava pushed up from under the sea. Life forms are slowly becoming established on this island, giving scientists a rare opportunity to study the creation of new land.

An eruption in the same area occurred on the island of Heimaey in 1973. A volcano exploded without warning, threatening to cover Heimaey in lava and ash. The entire population was evacuated to safety by boats.

The volcano continued to pour forth lava for five months, sending out 33 million tons (30 million metric tons) of debris. The flow threatened to block the island's harbor. In an attempt to forestall this, at the suggestion of a physicist named Thorbjörn Sigurgeirsson, cold sea water was sprayed onto the 500-foot- (150-m-) high wall of lava, which was advancing at 100 feet (30 m) per day. This may have helped to stop the flow. The wall of lava eventually halted 500 feet (150 m) short of blocking the harbor entrance. A third of the town was buried under the lava, while the size of the island expanded by 15 percent. Instead of blocking the harbor, the lava created a more sheltered entrance.

Geological activity is evident in other features besides the eruption of volcanoes. Near the volcanoes are areas of hot ground, known as solfataras, where vents emit hot gases or vapors. Underground heating results in hot springs. At places, when enough pressure builds, these hot springs spout forth jets of hot water. Great Geyser used to spout regularly to a height of 200 feet (60 m) but is now largely dormant, surprising many when it last erupted in June 2001. Others in the same area still spout, however, including Strokkur, which erupts every few minutes, spewing out hot water to a height of up to 100 feet (30 m).

The energy contained in geological hot spots has been extensively harnessed by Icelanders. Hot water is piped to provide heated swimming pools in most Icelandic communities. More advanced technologies are used to heat most buildings with geothermal energy piped in from these "hot spots."

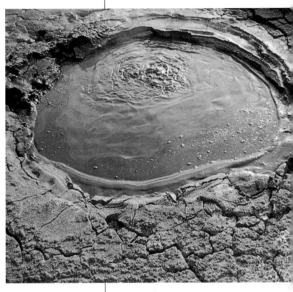

Solfataras and pools of bubbling hot mud are common sights in Iceland, especially in the south.

Much of Iceland is subject to strong winds and rain, both in summer and winter.

CLIMATE

The climate of Iceland is moderate. The warming effect of the Gulf Stream keeps temperatures in Reykjavík from falling much below freezing. The average January temperature in Reykjavík is 31°F (-0.6°C). Iceland's position in the northern North Atlantic prevents summers from getting hot. The average July temperature in Reykjavík is 52°F (11.2°C).

Reykjavík is exposed to the prevailing southwesterly winds blowing in from the Atlantic and as a result is subject to considerable rain. It averages three clear days in January, and only one entirely clear day in July! Rain and cloud cover are less relentless in other parts of Iceland. In the north and east the average summer temperature is warmer than Reykjavík, but winter temperatures are cooler.

In the northwest, snow falls on an average of 100 days a year, while the southeast averages about 40 snowy days per year. Strong winds are common throughout Iceland. In the *sandur* and some areas of the interior, dust storms make travel very difficult. Strong winds frequently close airports throughout Iceland, even the international airport at Keflavík.

THE NAMING OF ICELAND

The climate of Iceland is moderate for its northern latitude. Winters are mild enough that the sea almost never freezes. The country got its name, however, from the presence of drift ice in one of the northwestern fjords.

"There was a man named Flóki Vilgerdarson, who was a great Viking." So begins the story that explains the naming of the island as recounted in *Landnámabók*, the medieval account of the first settlers. Flóki set out from Norway with his companions, intending to settle in the newly discovered island. They included livestock among the provisions they took with them. They stayed for the summer in the western fjords and enjoyed the good fishing and seal-catching, but made no preparations to support their livestock through the winter. As a result, when winter came and snow covered the land, the animals died from lack of hay. In early spring, Flóki climbed a mountain to assess their prospects and looked out over a fjord full of ice. Discouraged, he named the island *Ísland*, meaning "ice land," and returned, after further misadventures, to Norway, where he spoke ill of the new country. One of his companions, Thorolf, however, stressed the bountiful nature of the new land. He claimed the country was so fertile that butter dripped off every blade of grass, and so he was nicknamed "Thorolf Butter."

LENGTH OF DAYS

Iceland is so far north that the length of the day varies greatly with the time of year. In summer, Iceland is a land of midnight sun; in winter, night never ends.

Strictly speaking, it is only on the island of Grímsey that the sun never sets (as seen from sea level) during the summer. Elsewhere in Iceland, only a brief period of twilight marks nights in June and July. Icelanders take full advantage of this period. Even little children tend to stay up late in the summer, when outdoor activities of all kinds are at a peak.

Conversely, in mid-winter daylight is limited to a few hours of twilight in the middle of the day. In the communities surrounded by steep fjords, particularly in the western fjords, the sight of the sun may be blocked throughout the winter until February or March. Icelanders tend to sleep more during the winter and many suffer from "short-day depression." The first sighting of the sun in the western fjords is greeted by a festival.

An Irish monk, in A.D. 825, commented that during summer the sun set only briefly, "so that no darkness occurs during that period of time, but whatever task a man wishes to perform, even picking the lice out of his shirt, he can manage it precisely as in broad daylight."

The almost total absence of trees is a common feature of the Icelandic landscape, contributing to an impression of bleakness.

Cold temperatures and strong winds make it hard for trees to grow. There have been attempts at reforestation, but what trees do grow tend to be stunted. A sign at one reforestation project even warns visitors not to step on the trees!

FLORA

When the first settlers arrived the island was covered in forests. Deforestation occurred so quickly that early Icelanders had to search for timber elsewhere, which led to the Viking discovery of North America. Soil erosion accompanied deforestation and was further aggravated by sheep grazing. Today, about a quarter of the country is covered by a continuous carpet of vegetation.

Mosses and lichens are the first plant life to appear on new lava fields. Nearly 500 types of moss and 450 types of lichen grow in Iceland. Marshes and bogs along the coastal wetlands support the growth of grasses and rushes. Blueberry and crowberry bushes grow on the heaths.

FAUNA

The only land mammal native to Iceland that predates human settlement is the arctic fox. Polar bears are rare visitors to Iceland; these animals occasionally drift across on pack ice from Greenland. A variety of rodents, including the rat and the mouse, were accidentally introduced into Iceland by settlers. Reindeer were introduced from Norway in the 18th century and now roam wild in the east of the country.

Seals are common; both harbor seals and gray seals breed on the coasts. Walruses are rare. Whales were once common, but hunting has made them less so. The killer whale, or orca, is now the most common, and there are occasional sightings of sperm, fin, humpback, and minke whales.

Iceland is a bird-watcher's paradise. About 70 species breed here, while another 230 species have been spotted. Inland birds include the gyrfalcon, a large falcon found only in Iceland; the white-tailed eagle, a bird of prey related to the American bald eagle; and the ptarmigan, a species of grouse hunted by both gyrfalcons and humans. There are many species of ducks, including eider, the sea-based duck whose feathers are valued for their warmth and softness in the making of eiderdown. Above all, there are vast colonies of sea birds, including gannets, fulmars, kittwakes, guillemots, and many more.

Seabirds nesting on cliffs off northern Iceland.

Three species of bird deserve special mention. The great auk was a large, flightless seabird that is now extinct. The last recorded specimen was killed in Iceland in 1844.

Puffins are Iceland's most common birds, with a population of 8 to 10 million. These small birds catch fish at sea and make nests by digging burrows into sea cliffs in huge communities. However, they are considered a delicacy by Icelanders and are hunted for food by puffin-catchers.

Arctic terns also nest extensively throughout Iceland. These birds migrate each winter from Antarctica, 10,000 miles away. If animals or people get too close to their nesting colonies, these birds protect their eggs and young by dive-bombing intruders, screeching the sound *kría*, which is their name in Icelandic.

An aerial view of the brightly colored roofs in Reykjavík, the capital city and commercial and cultural center of Iceland.

CITIES

REYKJAVÍK Reykjavík and its suburbs (with a total population of 187,263 as of the year 2006) are home to over half the population of Iceland. It is a clean, modern city, with a harbor and an airport, which handles domestic flights. The international airport is located in Keflavík, south of Reykjavík. Reykjavík is the cultural center of Iceland, boasting a symphony orchestra, theater, museum, and library, as well as amenities such as hotels and restaurants. It is the site of the university, the parliament, and the major cathedral.

Reykjavík is also the principal commercial and industrial center of Iceland. The region was first settled around 870. In the 18th century a village grew in the area and was granted municipal rights in 1786. Reykjavík was made the episcopal see in 1796, and the seat of the Althing (the Icelandic parliament) in 1843. In 1918 Reykjavík became the capital of Iceland. During World War II, the city was a British and U.S. naval and air base.

Residential homes in Reykjavík are generally built of concrete and sport brightly colored roofs. The city has improved its tourist facilities considerably in the hope that these improved amenities will attract more tourists to Iceland.

AKUREYRI Despite being Iceland's second largest city, Akureyri is a small town by European standards, with a population of only 16,736. Incorporated as a city in 1786, Akureyri is situated in the middle of the north coast, at the sheltered end of a long fjord. It is a major fishing harbor and also the center for tourism in the northern half of the country.

ÍSAFJÖRDUR Ísafjördur, with a population of 2,777, is the major town on the Vestfirdhir (the western fjords) peninsula. A picturesque small town centering on its harbor, it is located in a valley surrounded by steep mountains. Fishing and fish processing are the city's major economic activities.

In the 1930s, W.H. Auden wrote: "All things considered, I consider Iceland, apart from Reykjavík, a very nice land."

THE SELECTION AND NAMING OF REYKJAVÍK

One of the early settlers of Iceland, following the abortive attempt by Flóki and his companions, was Ingólfur Arnarson. Ingólfur set out with his family, slaves, and the trappings of his homestead in Norway, including his high seat, an ornately carved seat that was a sign of status. On reaching the coast of Iceland, he made a vow to Thor that he would settle wherever the pillars supporting his high seat washed ashore, and then cast the pillars into the water.

At first the pillars were not found and Ingólfur spent his first winter on the south coast (at a place now named Ingólfshöfdi). The following spring his slaves found the pillars. Ingólfur named the spot Reykjavík, meaning "Smoky Bay," on account of the steam rising from the geothermal springs. Here he built his homestead.

Reykjavík has retained its name to this day, even though it is probably one of the world's most smoke-free cities, due to its extensive use of clean, geothermal power.

HISTORY

ACCORDING TO HISTORICAL RECORDS, seafarers had some idea of the existence and position of Iceland as early as the fourth century. The first known inhabitants of Iceland were Irish religious recluses, who, in the ninth century, exploited the remoteness of the island to provide themselves with monastic seclusion. Early Norwegian settlers described seeing such individuals, who carried the accoutrements of their monastic profession in the form of bells and books and who kept away from the Norse settlers. Little else is known of these Irish hermits, except that they left when the permanent pagan (that is, the Norse) settlers began to arrive.

Icelandic institutions and culture flourished in medieval times until the country lost its independence and became subject first to Norway and then Denmark. For many centuries the prosperity of Iceland waned considerably. Independence was only recovered in 1944, and since that time Iceland has become strikingly prosperous once again.

Left: **A type of traditional Icelandic sod house.**

Opposite: **The Osvor Maritime Museum preserves the 19th century fishermen's huts at Bolungarvik in Iceland's western fjords region.**

THE AGE OF SETTLEMENT

Around A.D. 874, displaced Norwegians started to settle in Iceland. In Norway, King Harald Fairhair was extending his power throughout the country, which led to the exodus of those chieftains who did not want to be subject to the king. Norway also has limited farmland, so there was always need for new land to support a growing population. Other settlers were fleeing quarrels, feuds, or legal action.

These displaced Norwegians raided and settled in England, Scotland, Ireland, parts of France, and the Shetland, Orkney, and Faroe Islands. They either intermarried or made slaves of local people. Since they took their wives and slaves with them to Iceland, the earliest Icelanders were not just of Norwegian stock, but also of Celtic blood. The most notorious foreign slaves among the early settlers were the Irish slaves of Ingólfur Arnarson's brother, Hjörleifur. They rebelled and killed Hjörleifur and his supporters, then fled to remote islands off the south coast of Iceland, where Ingólfur tracked them down and killed them. The islands are now called Vestmannæyjar (or Westmann Islands), meaning "Islands of the People from the West."

It has been estimated that 20,000 people moved to Iceland between 874 and 930. By 930, most of Iceland's habitable land had been claimed. Until the end of the 10th century, landholdings were large. Each homestead contained many people and was practically a self-supporting economic unit. Initially, the settlers lived mostly by fishing, but sheep farming soon became the second most important industry.

Ingólfur Arnarson, the first settler of Iceland (memorialized in this statue), was involved in a feud over who would marry his sister, which led him and his foster brother, Hjörleifur Hrodmarsson, to kill a potential suitor. It was because of this feud that Ingólfur left Norway for Iceland.

ESTABLISHMENT OF THE ALTHING

In 930 the first nationwide parliament in Iceland, known as the Althing, was established. Local regional assemblies, called *things* (things), had already been established for the arbitration of disputes between settler families. Each *thing* was presided over by a local chieftain. The chieftains founded a national parliament and a high court (collectively known as the Althing), and adopted a general system of laws for the entire country. The Althing became the supreme authority of the land, presided over by a lawspeaker and by the chieftains of the island. It served to arbitrate disputes and to provide a social and commercial focus. It met every year in the summer for two weeks at Thingvellir. The event had something of a carnival air. Goods were traded, stories were recited, and marriages were arranged between families.

Although the idea for the local *thing* came from Norway, the Althing was unique in medieval Europe because it imposed centralized authority through group consensus rather than through the power of a king. Iceland was exceptional—a medieval nation that lacked a king. Icelanders say the Althing was the first legislative assembly in northern Europe.

An aerial view of the site of the Althing on the plain of Thingvellir, located on the shore of Thingvallavatn, Iceland's largest lake. The rock formations at Thingvellir form a natural amphitheater, making it an ideal natural site for the first legislative assembly in northern Europe.

A stone marker now marks the site of the law rock.

SOCIAL AND LEGAL BUSINESS Legal proceedings were held at the law rock. The chief organizer there was the lawspeaker, who was responsible for reciting from memory one third of the laws each year, so that all people should know the law, even if they could not read.

At the law rock, cases were presented before judges appointed by chieftains. The judgment process was not entirely just because the complexities of the law often led to a case being decided on technicalities. There was no police force to carry out judgments, so they were enforced by the chieftains. This made it hard to carry out a judgment against those chieftains.

If a judgment was considered unfair, a feud was likely to develop. Medieval Icelanders considered vengeance the most natural form of justice. The support of chieftains was very important for security against such quarrels. There were 36 (later 39) chieftains, known as *godi* (GO-thi). These *godar* (GO-thahr) also acted as pagan priests. People could choose which *godi* to follow and the power of the *godi* could be passed on or exchanged.

The other members of society were farmers, their wives, and their families. Women could own property and be considered the head of the household only when widowed. Given the many violent feuds, this often occurred. Children were educated in the household and were put to work on the farm at an early age. Farmers also kept slaves, although slavery gradually died out. Freed slaves became poor laborers who had to support themselves during the harsh winters.

THE VIKINGS

Vikings got their name from their raiding activity along the coast of the North Sea and farther inland. *Viking* was probably derived from the Old English *wician* (WEEK-ian), meaning "to camp," in reference to the temporary camps of the raiders. Young men from Norway and Denmark found that it was highly profitable to sail off for adventure and plunder in surrounding lands during the summer. Monasteries were easy targets, since these were full of valuable objects and wholly undefended.

As Viking raids on England intensified in the 10th and 11th centuries, English kings tried to buy off the Viking leaders by paying them tribute. On occasion this ran to huge sums of money. The Anglo-Saxon Chronicle records that in 1018 the English paid £82,500. Most of this money was paid in pennies, the standard coinage of the day. Scholars of English coins can find more examples of English coins of this period in Denmark and Norway than in England.

THE SAGA AGE

The nature of society changed somewhat with the coming of Christianity in A.D. 1000. The first missionaries caused disputes and much bloodshed by slandering the heathen gods. In A.D. 1000 the choice between Christianity and paganism was put in the hands of the lawspeaker, Thorgeir, who pondered the issue at the law rock for a day and a night. Thorgeir finally declared that all people should follow one law and that law should be the law of Christianity, although with continuing tolerance for paganism.

Icelanders of the Middle Ages were significant travelers. Many prominent Icelanders journeyed to Norway for trade and adventure, where the sagas depict them as generally well-received by Norwegian kings. They also traveled to England and continental Europe and discovered new lands to the west. Erik the Red was exiled from Iceland because of a killing and went west to discover a large ice-covered island, which he named Greenland to entice further settlers. He succeeded in leading Icelanders to settle there and two major settlements remained for several hundred years. Erik's son, Leif, sailed west, intending to explore the North American coast, which had been discovered by chance and bad navigation by a sailor bound for Greenland. Leif sailed the northeast shore of what is now Canada until he was far enough south to find grapes growing. He thus named the land *Vínland*, meaning "wine-land."

Some scholars think "Viking" comes from the word vik, *which means "bay." The idea was that the pirates are those who wait in the bay to raid passing ships.*

A popular tourist spot, Snorri's pool is named for Snorri Sturluson, who wrote *The History of the Kings of Norway*. Slain on the orders King Håkon of Norway, the great saga writer died like a character in a saga.

THE STURLUNGA AGE

Decline from the heights of the Saga Age came about through the concentration of power in the hands of fewer and fewer chieftains in the 13th century. One of the most powerful families of this time were the descendants of Hvamm-Sturla, thus this period is named Sturlunga (*Sturlunga* means "children of Sturla").

Snorri Sturluson was one of the most powerful chieftains. He was also an important saga writer, who wrote *The History of the Kings of Norway*. He built up his wealth and power through marriage and was a skillful political operator who was twice elected lawspeaker. He helped maintain his own power in Iceland through friendship with the king of Norway, Håkon.

In 1241 Snorri broke away from King Håkon, who wanted to extend his power over Iceland. Håkon employed a rival chieftain, Gizurr Thorvaldsson, to go after Snorri. Despite the fact that Gizurr had been Snorri's son-in-law, Gizurr pursued Snorri. A large force caught Snorri at home in the middle of the night on September 22, 1241. Snorri tried to escape to a secret hideout built under the kitchen but was betrayed by a servant and assassinated.

Icelandic independence ended in 1262. Such anarchy had broken out that the Althing gave King Håkon the right to collect taxes from Icelanders in return for imposing order. Iceland became a colony of Norway. Thus began a long decline in Iceland's independence and prosperity.

COLONIAL STATUS

Upon the loss of independence, Icelandic *godi* were replaced by royal officials who enforced the law of the Norwegian king. The king imposed a monopoly on trade and Iceland became dependent on unreliable Norwegian traders. To make matters worse, volcanic eruptions devastated Iceland.

In 1380 the balance of power shifted among the Scandinavian nations and Norway came under the control of Denmark. Iceland became a colony of Denmark and the trade monopoly was passed to the Danish king. Consequently, imported goods had to be bought at the high price imposed by the Danish, who in turn paid low prices for Icelandic fish.

In the middle of the 16th century, during the Protestant Reformation, Lutheranism was imposed on Iceland by the Danish king. The Althing lacked significant authority and was abolished by the Danish king in 1800. Meanwhile, volcanic eruptions and earthquakes took their toll yet again.

When Denmark sided with Napoleon at the beginning of the 19th century, its influence declined. The British navy defeated the Danish fleet, and in 1807 the British attacked the seat of the Danish government in Copenhagen. In 1809, Jorgen Jorgensen, a Danish interpreter for would-be British traders, temporarily liberated Iceland from Danish rule. He captured the Danish governor, imprisoned him on a British warship, and declared Iceland's independence. Jorgensen's overthrow of Danish rule was reversed on the arrival of a second British warship two months later.

The face of Satan, part of the scene of the *Last Judgment*, from a 12th-century wooden panel from Hólar Cathedral.

This statue of Jón Sigurdsson, the Father of Icelandic independence, stands proudly in a square in downtown Reykjavík. Iceland was declared independent on his birthday.

INDEPENDENCE

Demands for home rule and independence increased during the 19th century as nationalists led by Jón Sigurdsson pressed for total independence. In 1874 the Althing was constitutionally guaranteed consultative status.

Home rule was introduced in 1904. Iceland became a sovereign state with its own flag in 1918, but remained subject to Denmark.

Severance from Denmark came during World War II. Iceland was of considerable strategic value to both sides. Its position in the middle of the North Atlantic made it a potentially useful base for shipping and for submarines. It could provide an airbase for planes needing to refuel while crossing the Atlantic.

In May 1940, the British occupied Iceland to preempt a German invasion and to secure this strategically important island. When the United States entered the war, the British force was replaced by 60,000 U.S. troops, equal to half of the population of Iceland at that time.

Icelanders resented the presence of the troops, but discovered that it brought economic benefits. Building projects, including the airport at Keflavík, provided income and jobs. Prices for Icelandic fish escalated.

The Icelandic government declared its intention to push for total independence, a move overwhelmingly approved in a national referendum. On June 17, 1944, at the traditional site of the Althing, Sveinn Björnsson, soon to become Iceland's first president, declared Iceland independent. Iceland had finally regained independence after 700 years.

CONTROVERSY OVER NATO AND THE U.S. BASE

Most Icelanders want to maintain international political neutrality. Accordingly, the Althing declined U.S. requests for 99-year leases on three bases in Iceland following World War II. In 1946 Iceland negotiated an agreement that entailed the withdrawal of U.S. troops within six months. Permission was granted, however, for the United States to use the airbase at Keflavík.

The post-World War II beginnings of the Cold War led to the establishment of the North Atlantic Treaty Organization (NATO). Iceland was persuaded to become a founding member in 1949. Membership in NATO has been a significant issue of contention between Iceland's political parties ever since. The issue was exacerbated in 1951, when U.S. forces established a permanent marine base at the airport at Keflavík. The Icelandic government threatened to close the base in 1973 but reversed its position a year later. The issue became pressing again when contingency plans to house nuclear weapons at Keflavík were released. The Althing declared Iceland a nuclear-free zone and the United States backed down.

The U.S. forces based in Iceland have thus assured Iceland's border defense for decades. However, in March 2006, the United States said that it will be withdrawing its bases from Iceland before the end of the year, bringing with it valuable F-15 fighters and thousands of servicemen, leaving Iceland without any armed forces. Although the United States has pledged to still defend Iceland, albeit from a distance, Iceland is now grappling with the decision as to whether it needs to arm itself militarily.

U.S. Marines building the base at Keflavík during World War II.

An Icelandic gunboat engaging a British fishing trawler during the height of the cod wars.

THE COD WARS

Iceland's economy and its prosperity in modern times has been heavily dependent on fishing— mainly on catching cod. Iceland's only international conflicts have revolved around this industry—in particular, over the size of Iceland's exclusive offshore fishing limits.

In 1952 Iceland declared exclusive right to fish in its offshore waters for a distance of 4 miles from the coast, an extension over the original 3-mile fishing limit. Britain, whose fleet also fished in these waters, protested and organized a ban on importing Icelandic fish, but the expanded zone remained in force. In 1958 Iceland expanded its exclusive fishing zone to 12 miles, then to 50 miles in 1972, and finally to 200 miles in 1975. On each occasion, Britain protested the expansion. Both nations patrolled the waters with gunboats to enforce their point. The British deployed the Royal Navy to try to protect British trawlers, while Iceland retaliated with Fisheries' Protection Vessels. These used huge clippers to cut the nets from offending trawlers. Tensions ran high, but there were no fatalities on either side.

The 200-mile limit was finally accepted by Britain in 1976, when it promptly created a 200-mile limit of its own. The countries agreed to compromise, with quotas for fishing in each other's waters. Iceland's position on fishing zones prevailed in the United Nations Draft Convention on the Law of the Sea and has become an internationally recognized standard.

Iceland's 200-mile limit created an overlap in the Barents Sea known as the "Herring loophole" with Norway's offshore limit. An agreement was reached on this area in 1980, but conflicts over the precise scope of each country's limits dragged on for years until Iceland, Norway, and Russia signed an agreement in 1999 letting Iceland fish in Russia's and Norway's Exclusive Economic Zone in exchange for certain benefits on Icelandic waters. Iceland, together with the United Kingdom and Ireland, is also in an ongoing dispute with Denmark over the latter's claim that the Faroe Islands' fisheries extend beyond the 200-mile line, disputing the Danish fishing boats' rights to operate in the area. ·

DIPLOMATIC INITIATIVES

Icelandic neutrality and its medial location between the United States and the Soviet Union made it a suitable location for the summit meeting between Presidents Ronald Reagan and Mikhail Gorbachev in 1986. The leaders met to discuss nuclear disarmament in a significant step toward ending the Cold War.

In the same tradition, Iceland became the first country to reestablish diplomatic relations with Estonia, Latvia, and Lithuania on August 26, 1991. The move helped give these early breakaway republics legitimacy and contributed to the break up of the Soviet Union.

Iceland believes in the protection of human rights, and has actively lent its support for peacekeeping missions. Bosnia, Kosovo, and Iraq have all benefited from Iceland's expertise and aid in reconstruction work. Icelandic aircraft were loaned out for the NATO mission in Afghanistan for airlifting supplies and peacekeeping forces.

Former U.S. President Ronald Reagan *(left)* and former Soviet Premier Mikhail Gorbachev *(right)* during their Reykjavík summit to discuss nuclear disarmament.

GOVERNMENT

ICELAND CAN CLAIM TO BE the first democractic state in northern Europe with the establishment of the Althing at Thingvellir in A.D. 930. Yet for most of its history Iceland has been a colony, first of Norway, and later, of Denmark.

Iceland began its steps toward independence in the early 20th century, with Denmark granting it home rule in 1904. The present Icelandic Constitution and institutions of government date from the declaration of independence in 1944. Despite the relative youth of the current democratic institutions, Iceland is a stable democratic nation.

Opposite: **Icelandic flags flying in front of the City Hall.**

Below: **The state Lutheran Church at Besstandir with the official residence of the president behind it.**

31

FOR AUDIO, VIDEO OR TRANSCRIPT: 1·800·NPC·2334

NATIONAL PRESS CLUB

Olafur Ragnar Grimsson, the president of Iceland since 1996, speaking at the National Press Club on "Democracy and Security in the New Millennium: A View from Iceland and the Country of Creation."

ELECTORAL SYSTEM

Iceland is governed by an elected president and an elected parliament. All citizens over 18 are entitled to vote both for president and members of parliament.

The president of Iceland is primarily a constitutional figurehead. A president is elected for a four-year term and may stand for reelection. He or she represents the country but is much less powerful than, for example, the president of the United States. The president of Iceland cannot simply veto legislation passed by parliament. If the president rejects a piece of legislation, that bill would go to a referendum. Rather than participating in day-to-day politics, the president acts as a unifying figure.

Parliament is known as the Althing to maintain continuity with the earliest parliament. The Althing, which meets in Reykjavík, consists of 63 members elected to four-year terms through a mixture of constituency and proportional representation. The Althing enacts all legislation and passes the annual budget.

The executive function of government is carried out by a cabinet, led by a prime minister. The current prime minister is Halldór Ásgrímsson. The prime minister is the leading political figure, like the prime minister of most Western European countries. The present cabinet has 12 ministers.

In addition to national representation, there are also elected officials at the regional and local levels. Local government carries most of the responsibility for education, municipal services, and health services. It also looks after the unemployed and poor through job-creation programs.

PARTY POLITICS

Deputies to the Althing are divided by political party. There is a tradition of coalition governments since one party rarely has enough representatives to give it an overall majority in government.

The largest single party is currently the Independence Party, with 22 deputies. This has traditionally been the strongest party and has participated in most governments since independence. The party draws strength from the electorate in and around Reykjavík. It stands for a liberal economic policy, economic stabilization, and continued NATO membership.

The Progressive Party is the current coalition partner of the Independence Party, with 12 deputies in the Althing. The chairperson of the party, Halldór Ásgrímsson, is currently the prime minister. The Progressive Party was originally founded as an agrarian party, particularly concerned about the interests of agriculture and fisheries but has since adopted the position of the liberal party, supporting continued membership in NATO.

The largest opposition party is the Social Democratic Alliance with 20 deputies in the Althing. Ingibjörg Sólrún Gísladóttir is the chairman of this party which merged with the People's Alliance, Social Democratic Party and Women's List to counter the Independence Party.

The fourth largest is the Left–Green Alliance with five deputies. This party focuses on traditional social values and environmentalism. The fifth-largest party is the Liberal Party with four deputies. It advocates a staunchly neutralist position in foreign affairs and opposes European Union (EU) membership.

Some of Iceland's members of the Althing at work in the Althing house.

33

THE WOMEN'S ALLIANCE

Women's issues are prominent in the Althing due to the existence of *Kvennalista* (KVEN-eh-list-eh), the Women's List or the Women's Alliance. This party was formed before the 1983 election to press for action on issues such as child care and equal opportunity for women. It won three deputies in the Althing. In keeping with the egalitarian ideals of the party, there was no formal leadership: the role of parliamentary leader rotated among its elected deputies.

Despite the existence of *Kvennalista*, in 1995 only one cabinet position was held by a woman. This caused an uproar and the ruling Independence Party assigned four women cabinet ministers the following term. Although the *Kvennalista* disbanded in 1999, its remaining members have since formed the Alliance coalition.

Ingibjörg Sólrún (in red), the former mayor of Reykjavík, was a *Kvennalista* member.

A WELFARE STATE

Since World War II, the Icelandic government has played a major part in the well-being of its citizens through a carefully developed welfare system. The state provides old-age and disability pensions for the elderly and infirm, along with benefits for childbearing and for sickness. Ninety percent of Icelandic workers belong to unions, which offer benefits such as guaranteed support in the event of unemployment.

Health insurance is compulsory for all citizens and all medical and hospital services are provided entirely without charge. The rate of infant mortality in Iceland is the lowest in the world, and an effective public health-care system helps to contribute to the longevity of the Icelandic population. Women have an average life expectancy of 82.7 years and men of 79.2, both of which are almost the highest in the world.

Senior citizens in Iceland do not have to worry about making ends meet or about the cost of health care because the state takes care of their needs in these areas.

A GUARANTEED WELFARE SYSTEM

Certain minimum guarantees for public welfare are provided for in the Constitution of Iceland. Articles 70 and 71 read: "Whoever is unable to provide for himself or his dependants shall, subject to duties prescribed by law, be entitled to support from public funds, unless his maintenance rests upon others. If parents cannot afford to educate their children, or if the children are orphaned or destitute, their education and maintenance must be defrayed from public funds."

ECONOMY

THE ECONOMY OF ICELAND since the Middle Ages has been deeply dependent on fish. Since World War II, Iceland has been a highly prosperous nation through exploiting the riches of the surrounding seas. Although fishing is the mainstay of the Icelandic economy, in recent times this resource has been threatened by over-fishing.

Iceland's other major resource is its vast supply of geothermal energy. This can be tapped in various ways, from heating homes to providing cheap energy for factories. The natural beauty of the island also makes it an obvious site for tourism.

Opposite: **Fishermen at Akureyri in northern Iceland hang their fish out to dry.**

Below: **A Swiss aluminum-smelter plant operating in Iceland. Smelting uses a vast amount of electricity. This economic development is controversial because of the potential for pollution from such heavy industry.**

Most Icelanders are avid consumers, fond of owning the newest models of cell phones.

COST OF LIVING

The cost of living in Iceland is very high. Most goods have to be imported and the tiny size of the population means that there are no economies of scale. Iceland's extensive social services are supported by high taxation, which further pushes up the cost of living.

Despite the high cost of living, Icelanders generally buy many high-priced goods and live an affluent lifestyle. There are more cars and VCRs per person in Iceland than in any country except the United States.

Cell phones and personal computers are also very popular. More than 84 percent of Icelanders are connected to the Internet. When a consumer item becomes a craze in Iceland, everybody wants to buy one.

Icelanders support their high standard of living by working long and hard; they put in the longest workweek in Europe. More than 80 percent of adult Icelandic women work outside the home.

Unemployment has traditionally been very low, with a rate of under 1 percent through most of the 1980s. Although the unemployment rate increased to 5.3 percent in late 1993, it has since steadily dropped over the years to 2.7 percent in 2005.

VARIETIES OF FISH

Iceland's waters are very rich in fish because many different species breed where the cold waters of the Arctic mix with the warm waters of the Gulf Stream. The different varieties of fish can be categorized by the environment in which they live in the ocean. Icelandic fishing fleets catch such bottom-feeding fish as cod, haddock, redfish, ocean catfish, Greenland halibut, and plaice, and top-water fish such as herring and capelin. They also catch fish that are on their way to freshwater rivers to breed, such as salmon, trout, and Arctic charr. Shellfish such as shrimps, scallops, and Norway lobsters are also part of the catch.

FISHING

The economic life of Iceland still depends on fish. Although fishing and fish processing employ only about 8 percent of the labor force, fish products provide 70 percent of Iceland's exports. The major fish catches are cod and haddock—exported either frozen, salted, or fresh—and capelin and herring, which are usually reduced to oil and meal.

Icelanders sell their fish to markets in North America and Europe. Nutrition studies stressing the health benefits of a fish diet that is naturally high in protein and low in cholesterol have helped ensure high demand. This demand is also boosted by the mad cow disease and bird flu scares as people are wary of tainted red meat and poultry.

However, intensive modern fishing methods have threatened Iceland's fish stocks. The government acted to protect stocks through an expansion of the exclusive fishing zone, now at 200 nautical miles, to prevent over-fishing by rival nations. It also imposed strict quotas. Icelandic vessels are given quotas based on the previous year's catch and the government's assessment of fish stocks of each species. These quotas are tradable, which has made fishermen develop the skills of futures traders who need to speculate with the canniness of accountants. The system won praise from the Organization of Economic and Community Development, which commented that "the tradable-quota system is an elegant and equitable means to achieve an efficient allocation of output."

Since an Icelander can only buy a new boat when replacing an old one, Iceland now has the most technologically advanced fishing fleet in the world. Successful fishermen, prohibited from expanding their operations, spend money on acquiring the latest technology and upgrading their vessels instead.

"Life is saltfish."

— *Halldór Laxness, Icelandic novelist*

A whale being cut up at a whale-processing station in Hvalfjördur.

WHALING

Whaling traditionally occupied a significant part of Iceland's economy. The whales were harpooned and brought to whale-processing stations on the coast, where the blubber was stripped and the carcass processed into meat and oil.

As whale stocks became over-exploited in the 1980s, the International Whaling Commission called for a voluntary temporary moratorium on all whaling. Iceland, however, along with Japan, insisted on continuing with limited whaling.

As public sentiment through most of the world turned in favor of a complete cessation of whaling, Iceland (and Japan and Norway) became more isolated because of their pro-whaling stance. In the mid-1980s environmental activists belonging to Greenpeace took direct action against the whaling industry: they sank an Icelandic ship and destroyed other whaling equipment.

WHALE STRANDINGS

Whales have sporadically stranded themselves on Icelandic beaches since earliest times. These beachings were considered a significant windfall for a district. Local farmers would descend on the whale and flense it — that is, remove the blubber from the skeleton. The blubber was cut into strips, which were hung under a bridge or from the eaves of a house. The meat would be left to mature, turning black, until it was ready to eat.

There would often be disputes over who had a right to a beached whale. Legally, such drift-finds were the property of the owner of the land. In *Grettir's Saga*, such a dispute arises while the finders are flensing a finwhale discovered at Rifsker. The dispute turns nasty:

"Thorgeir Bottleback was the first to get on to the whale where Flósi's men were. Thorfinn was cutting it up, standing near the head on the place where he had been carving. 'Here I bring you your ax,' said Thorgeir. Then he struck at Thorfinn's neck and cut off his head."

The following verse was composed about these events:

Hard were the blows which were dealt at Rifsker;
No weapons they had but steaks of the whale.
They belabored each other with rotten blubber.
Unseemly methinks is such warfare for men.

Most Icelanders were appalled by this act of deliberate sabotage. Fishermen resented having their livelihood taken away because of what they considered sentimental attachment to an animal. City dwellers were more likely to be sympathetic to whales, but still resented foreign meddling in Icelandic affairs. Nevertheless, U.S. boycotts of Icelandic fish products threatened to do real damage to the Icelandic economy and encouraged a moderation of Iceland's whaling position.

Although Iceland still believes it has the right to conduct whaling in its waters, it guaranteed to restrict whaling operations to "research whaling," in which whaling was conducted only for scientific purposes and most of the products from the whales were not exported for commercial purposes. In 1989, however, even this limited whaling was suspended. Fourteen years later, controversy arose over the government's decision to conduct scientific whaling to investigate the impact of whales on fish stocks. In 2003 Iceland resumed whaling with quotas set and permits issued for scientific catches.

The major activity of Icelandic farmers is raising sheep. There are twice as many sheep in Iceland as people. Sheep graze on mountainside vegetation during the summer. At this time, farmers cultivate grass in the valleys, which they harvest in the fall to provide hay for the sheep through the winter. Rounding up the sheep from the highlands is a fall tradition.

FARMING

Today only 3.4 percent of Icelanders are employed on 3,800 farms, and agriculture accounts for 2 percent of Icelandic exports. Employment in the farm sector shrank by 23 percent between 1980 and 1990. Nevertheless, many Icelanders have a nostalgic fondness for farming, recalling a time earlier in the 20th century when most people lived and worked on farms. Government policy strongly favors farmers; as a result food is very costly for consumers.

Sheep farming is the most important agricultural industry in the country. Dairy farming is also significant.

Despite the northern climate, vegetables are grown in Iceland—in greenhouses heated by geothermal energy. The varieties grown include cabbages, lettuce, carrots, and tomatoes. These crops benefit from Iceland's long summer days. Practically all fruit, along with other vegetables, has to be imported.

THERMAL ENERGY

The geological activity that is so visible throughout Iceland represents a potential economic resource and creates a setting of stark beauty. Iceland has harnessed various forms of geothermal energy to provide cheap heat and power for homes and industry. The Reykjavík municipality currently uses this inexpensive, clean form of energy to provide central heating for all city households. Since most heat is tapped from seismic activity beneath the earth's surface, it is not necessary to burn much oil or other hydrocarbons as fuel, thus no environmentally harmful greenhouse gases are produced. All the same, only a small fraction of potentially exploitable geothermal power is currently harnessed.

Iceland's rivers provide hydroelectric power, but only a small fraction of the energy that could be exploited has been developed. In view of the potential for further clean electricity production through geothermal and hydroelectric generation, there is currently a plan to export electricity to Europe. This involves an ambitious plan to build the longest submarine electric cable in the world under the Atlantic Ocean from Iceland to Britain, and even to Germany, at an estimated cost of $4.9 million.

One geothermal project near Keflavík has had a surprising spin-off. Superheated salt water is pumped from deep in the earth and used to generate electricity. It then passes through a heat exchanger to provide hot fresh water for heating homes. The mineral-rich saltwater from the earth finally runs off into a pool named the Blue Lagoon for its color. Those who bathe in these warm waters claim to have been cured of various skin complaints.

Bathing in the Blue Lagoon is now a popular tourist activity.

43

Ice fishing on Lake Myvatn is a popular activity for both locals and tourists.

TOURISM

Iceland was an exotic destination for European travelers in the 19th century, and many of them wrote accounts of their travels. Tourism has become increasingly popular and now constitutes a significant part of Iceland's economic activity. In 1950, 4,000 tourists visited Iceland; in 2004 there were 360,000 visitors.

Tourists are brought to Iceland by Icelandair, the national airline and a budget airline, the Iceland Express. Cheap fares across the Atlantic gave passengers the opportunity to stop over for short vacations in Iceland. These days increasing numbers of tourists are seeking out Iceland as a principal vacation destination. The other way of getting there is by car ferry from Denmark, Norway, Scotland, or the Faroe Islands.

Tourists are drawn above all by the natural beauty of this island and by the resonance of its historic sites. Three of the major tourist sites—the site of the early parliament at Thingvellir, the Gullfoss waterfall, and the active geysers around Geysir—are easily accessible from Reykjavík.

Iceland is particularly suited to outdoor pursuits. Hikers can walk in the unpopulated interior. Equestrians can explore on Iceland's distinctive small horses. And anyone can relax after their exertions by swimming in the pools heated by geothermal water.

Recreational fishing is popular in Icelandic rivers but is regulated to preserve fish stocks and maximize revenue. Fishing can be expensive—a permit for fishing in the best salmon rivers can cost $1,300 per day!

Another expanding area for tourism is the opportunity to live on a farm. "Tourist farming" has been gladly embraced by some farmers as an additional opportunity for diversification. As Icelandic farms become less economic for producing food, farmers are able to capitalize on the nostalgia for a rural lifestyle by opening up their farms to tourists who pay to take part in such activities as rounding up the sheep.

In recent times, Iceland has been marketing itself as an ideal "green" tourist and whale watching destination. The island's particularly clean air and water and the use of geothermal energy rather than the burning of hydrocarbons is a source of pride for Icelanders. The government has stated its objective "that Iceland be, by the turn of the century, the cleanest country in the Western world and that an image of cleanliness and sustainability be associated with all developments."

Professional and amateur ornithologists are well served by the cliffs teeming with bird life, especially at Hornstrandir or on the Westmann Islands.

ENVIRONMENT

IN COMPARISON TO MOST nations, Iceland suffers relatively little environmental pollution. This in part explains the somewhat inadequate public awareness regarding environmental conservation. It was only in the 1950s that Iceland began to take affirmative action in conserving its environment.

The first Nature Conservation Act was passed in 1956. In 1990 the Ministry of Environment was established. Some of the ministry's concerns include the prevention and control of pollution, and the preservation of nature.

One of Iceland's main environmental challenges is the full utilization of its natural resources, like thermal energy and marine resources, without compromising their sustainability. This sometimes makes policies difficult to implement as at times economic needs transcend environmental considerations. One such example would be the construction of a hydroelectric plant for smelting aluminium in an area of unspoiled beauty.

In 2002 the government formulated a strategy called Welfare for the Future to promote a sustainable environment and future, and also a greater quality of life for Icelanders.

Above: **Hot springs along the river valleys in south-west Iceland.**

Opposite: **Surrounded by lava cones and craters, Lake Myvatn is fed by geothermal springs. Its bio-rich waters never freeze and they provide a sanctuary for birds.**

MARINE CRISIS

The coastal zones of Iceland are of great economic value as 70 percent of Iceland's exports are from fish and fish manufacturing alone. The majority of Icelanders also live near the coast, so the preservation of Iceland's

A bubbling hot spring at the Geysir geothermal field near Reykjavík.

waters is a sound social and economic move. Iceland does not suffer from much water pollution as laws and regulations ensure that pollution is kept to a minimum.

There are numerous environmental bodies in charge of protection and conservation of marine resources for sustainable use. Although there is no marine ecosystem currently in danger, checks are already in place to pre-empt an ecological imbalance. The relevant bodies make sure that the dumping of waste products off fishing fleets, oil spills, and the transportation of hazardous chemicals are kept tightly in check. Even the types of fishing gear and mesh sizes of nets used are strictly regulated. Quotas are imposed to prevent over-fishing and penalties are levied for illegal catches. This is to prevent the depletion of fish stocks, especially since particular species of fish of high commercial value tended to be over-fished.

The government has also banned the use of chemicals containing mercury, arsenic, and organotins on its waters. Currently there are four types of protected areas in the coastal zone. Depending on the area, trawl fishing is prohibited in protected coastal waters. Protected areas may also be closed off for long periods to protect young fishes, certain species of fish, or the ecosystem. During the spawning season, the area may be closed off for a short period of time. If the Marine Research Institute sees fit, it can also cordon off certain areas to prevent damage to fishing stocks and ecosystems.

With so many checks put in place, it comes as a surprise that Iceland is still lacking the infrastructure to prevent fertilizer run-off into the sea from agricultural practices. However, there have not been any marked changes in Iceland's waters, perhaps because only 1 percent of Icelandic land is cultivated for agricultural purposes.

In 1995 a marine conservation area was set up in Breidafjordur, West Iceland. The purpose of this facility is to oversee the sustainability of fisheries and ecological conservations. With the local community also involved in the programs, there has been increased awareness and interest in the preservation of Icelandic waters. In conjunction with the International Year of the Ocean, children and youth are educated on the sustainability of Icelandic fisheries. On-site visits to harbors are very popular with both the youth and adults.

Fishing boats at the dry dock facility in Hafnarfjördur harbor.

The receding Vatnajökull glacier in southeast Iceland.

GLOBAL WARMING

In late 2004, more than 200 scientists and researchers from the Arctic Council released an alarming report on rising temperatures in the Arctic. The increase in the earth's average temperature, or global warming, is largely due to the burning of fossil fuels, which releases greenhouse gases. According to the report, there has been an increase in the water levels in the Arctic because of melting ice caps. Over the last 30 years, almost 386,100 square miles (999,995 square km) of sea ice has melted and the average winter temperature of the Artic today has increased by 35.6°F (2°C) compared to a century ago. Vatnajökull, the largest glacier in southeast Iceland is fast receding due to global warming. Melting at the rate of 3 feet (1 m) annually, it is estimated that in 300 years, Vatnajökull would completely disappear. Approximately 11 percent of Iceland is covered in glacial ice and permanent snow and 3,088 miles (4,970 km) of coastal waters surrounds Iceland. If global warming were to continue unchecked, the subsequent rise in water levels and melting of ice caps would be detrimental to Iceland.

Iceland ratified the Kyoto Protocol in 2002 limiting emissions of greenhouse gases. Further steps that Iceland hopes to take include boosting public transportation and limiting the number of private cars on the road. This is particularly important as heavy traffic in the Greater Reykjavík area is a cause of air pollution. Iceland also hopes to reduce the dependence on fossil fuels for the operation of its fishing vessels. Further technological research and developments in the field of clean sources of energy are necessary to help tackle the problem of global warming. As only 18 percent of Iceland's hydroelectric energy has been harnessed, Iceland has made plans to increase the use of this sustainable energy for power intensive industries.

THE IMPORTANCE OF RENEWABLE ENERGY

There are abundant renewable energy resources like hydropower and geothermal energy in Iceland. Geothermal energy makes up about

This geothermal plant at Krafla processes diatomaceous earth from the bottom of Lake Myvatn for industrial use.

54 percent and hydropower 18 percent of Iceland's energy use. The rest comes from imported fossil fuels. Today there are three major geothermal plants and seven hydropower plants. To promote full utilization of this energy source, long-term low interest loans will be given to small communities interested in developing geothermal energy for their needs.

Geothermal energy is used to power greenhouses and industry, and supply warm water for fish farming and swimming pools. It is estimated that the use of this energy will benefit more than 90 percent of Icelanders in the foreseeable future. This form of energy, however, produces waste water containing hazardous chemicals like boron, mercury, and arsenic, which if not disposed of properly, could pollute Iceland's waters.

However, the benefits of using geothermal energy far outweigh the negative effects. Compared to nuclear power plants, geothermal plants

A hydrogen fuel cell bus refuelling in a Shell station in Reykjavík.

do not deplete the ozone layer and have little negative impact on the environment if properly managed.

Currently Iceland is one of the leading countries in the world actively participating in research on using hydrogen as a renewable energy. Iceland is also one of the founding members of the International Partnership on the Hydrogen Economy (IPHE). Major stakeholders like Shell Hydrogen, Daimler Chrysler, and Hydro support a joint venture for the research and development of hydrogen as a renewable source of energy. To date, there are three successful hydrogen fuel cell buses in Reykjavík.

WASTE

Iceland has made slow but considerable progress in waste management. In the 1970s it was common to incinerate waste in an open pit and smoky open dumps were a common sight. In the 1990s incineration became less popular, with only 1.2 percent of waste being incinerated. Uncontrolled open pit burning was gradually stopped by the year 2000 as recycling became a more environmentally conscious option. Although incineration plants are still being used, some plants recycle waste matter to be reused as energy. However, only 3 percent of waste matter burned is recovered as energy. On the other hand, landfilling seems to be slow in losing popularity. In 1995, 80 percent of Icelandic waste was landfilled and in 2005, the number fell slightly lower to 71 percent.

New legislation on waste management seeks to address this pressing environmental problem. The goal of the law is to decrease the need to landfill waste, cut down on waste generation, and step up recycling and recovery programs. The law specifies that organic waste to be landfilled must be reduced by 25 percent before January 2009. Packaging waste needs to be recovered by 50 percent and at least 25 percent of packaging materials must be recycled.

Additionally, there will be a ban on landfilling scrap metals, hazardous waste, and radioactive and contagious waste. Landfill operators have to comply with the above regulations by July 2009 or face the termination of their services. It is likely that the cost of waste management will increase due to the new regulations. The situation will be closely monitored by the Coordination Committee whose role is to make certain that not only are the rules observed but that there will be adequate funding to ensure the successful implementation of the law.

At present, Reykjavík's waste treatment facility is provided by SORPA. SORPA also manages 62 percent of Iceland's total disposal needs. In main areas of the city, SORPA provides containers and bins free of charge for the collection of recyclable items, like paper and beverage containers. In 2002, Iceland managed to recover close to 30 percent and recycle 27 percent of their packaging goods like glass, plastic, and paper.

A GREENER ICELAND

Iceland's livelihood is dependent on its ability to sustain and fully utilize its natural resources. Fishery issues are important, and from 2002 to 2004 Iceland chaired the Artic Council promoting sustainable development and environmental protection in the Arctic. Iceland is also an active member of the UN Convention on the Law of the Sea. In 1998 Iceland set up the UN University Fisheries Training Programme on its homesoil, offering specialized postgraduate courses to participants from other countries, and sharing its knowledge and expertise on fisheries management and policies.

It is crucial that the reputation of Iceland's clean waters is maintained. Iceland seeks to further promote the sustainability of its oceans by adopting the Convention on Persistent Organic Pollutants protecting marine environment and diversity in 2003. The country also adheres to the Marpol Convention, monitoring dumping from ships and marine pollution from oil spills. Under the OSPAR Convention and the Bern Agreement, Iceland has stepped up its protection and preservation of wildlife habitats. It has also made plans to protect more of its wetlands as agreed under the Ramsar Convention.

Clean air is not taken for granted and Iceland is a party to the Convention on Long Range Transboundary Air Pollution whose aim is to gradually reduce and prevent air pollution regardless of borders. Iceland also plans to further reduce the emission of greenhouse gases from its fishing and transportation industries.

CONSERVATION OF NATURE

Much of Iceland's nature and wildlife habitat is under conservation and protection. There are four national parks and over 80 protected areas in Iceland. They are the Skaftafell National Park, Jökulsárgljúfur National Park, Thingvellir National Park, and a new addition in 2001 called Snaefellsjökull National Park. The government has decided that the massive Vatnajökull glacier and the areas flanking it should be protected. Some of the protected areas include Lake Myvatn, Gullfoss, and Surtsey among others. These parks are designed to keep Iceland's wildlife safe, conserve the area's unique landscape, and, at the same time, offer tourists and Icelanders alike a glimpse of Iceland's natural wilderness.

At Lake Myvatn alone, there are numerous duck species. One can find the tufted duck, the scaup, Barrow's goldeneye, and other rare species like the goosander, shoveller, and pochard. In Iceland all endangered or rare birds, like the gyrfalcon and the white tailed eagle, are protected by law. In 1926 there were only ten pairs of white tailed eagles in Iceland. Today there are 35 to 40 breeding pairs. Permission from the Ministry of Culture is needed if one wishes to photograph or approach the endangered birds' nesting places.

The conservation and protection of nature is important to Icelanders. Conservationists petitioned against a project to build a new aluminium smelter in eastern Iceland. They were concerned that the project would destroy the landscape. The Kárahnukar hydropower plant project has so far dammed two major glacial rivers north of Vatnajökull. The Icelandic Nature Conservation Association campaigned hard for the conservation of this area but this controversial project still proceeded. The construction of a new plant in Iceland will always be a source of contention and the benefits of progress must outweigh the cost to Iceland's environment. Iceland will have to balance the twin goals of full utilization of its natural resources with the preservation of its land and sea.

Puffins nesting on the sea cliffs of Heimaey Island.

ICELANDERS

THE POPULATION OF ICELAND is strikingly homogeneous. The original settlers were a mix of Nordic Vikings and Celtic slaves and wives. After a millennium of intermarriage, no distinctions between the two groups are evident any longer. The population is essentially Nordic in appearance: characteristically tall, blond-haired, and light-skinned.

Icelanders are generally strong and beautiful. In the last 10 years, Icelandic women have thrice won the Miss World competition. Beauty pageants and modelling contests are extremely popular in Iceland. Icelanders are slightly taller and heavier than the average for most nations.

Left: **Jón Páll Sigmarsson, was declared the Strongest Man of All Time in 1987 after winning the World's Strongest Man championship four times.**

Opposite: **An Icelandic girl in native costume at the Independence Day celebrations in Reykjavík.**

It is unusual to find a dark-haired Icelander, except among some teenagers who dye their hair to be different.

A HOMOGENOUS SOCIETY

Historically, there have been virtually no racial minorities in Iceland. In general, immigration into Iceland is heavily restricted and the number of immigrants has been very small. In any case, the largest number of immigrants come from other Nordic countries and have not contributed to diversifying the ethnic makeup of the country.

Icelanders' attitudes to people of other races is clouded by this lack of contact. When the U.S. base was first established at Keflavík in the 1950s, the Icelandic government insisted on a secret agreement that no black servicemen should be based there. This agreement has since ended. A 1989 survey found that a large majority of Icelanders thought that people of other races should settle in Iceland. In the 1980s, a number of Icelandic families responded to the Vietnamese refugee crisis by adopting orphaned children, who may begin to diversify Icelandic society. All the same, there is a distinctive name for immigrants who belong to different races, *nýbúar* (NEE-boo-ah), which literally means "new-dwellers," and such new-dwellers may experience the tensions and prejudices that arise from being visible outsiders trying to enter the close-knit fabric of Icelandic society.

Iceland's population is homogeneous in several other ways, too. All Icelanders speak the same language, with almost no regional or class dialects. Ninety-five percent of Icelanders are Lutheran, with 85.5 percent identifying with the state Church of Iceland.

The impression of homogeneity and the close-knit nature of Icelandic society is emphasized by the smallness of Iceland's population. When talking to Icelanders, one can get the impression that everyone knows everyone else, and talk soon turns to uncovering mutual acquaintances. Icelanders also have a strong sense of their heritage and genealogy. If no connection can be found in the present generation, it is often possible to trace ties in former generations.

One consequence of this small and close-knit sense of society is that Icelanders have a personal stake in the news. In a population of only a quarter of a million, over half of them in one urban area, there is a reasonable possibility that one will know personally anyone who is in the news. This creates a caring society in which almost everybody is famous in some way and their achievements talked about widely by the rest of society. It can also foster, however, a sense of subtle control since it is almost impossible to do anything without the deed being found out and discussed by one's peers.

The small size of the population has a major impact on the attitudes of Icelanders. They are cohesive and have a strong sense of community.

CLASS

Modern Iceland has inscribed something of its egalitarian nature in its Constitution. Article 78 states: "Privileges reserved for nobility, titles and rank must never be enacted." This is presumably a reaction to the class structure of Denmark, which has titled nobles as well as a monarch.

There is less social and economic stratification in Iceland than in most countries. The difference in wages between different professions is also smaller. Egalitarianism, the equality of all people, is widely recognized as an important ideal by all Icelanders. This spirit is encouraged, like so much else, by the small size of the population. In a close-knit society, where most people are known personally, it is harder to put on airs.

Icelanders can leave school at the age of 16 or continue their schooling until they are 20. There is a different level of expectation for those who leave school at the earliest opportunity. They are more likely to work in lower-skilled jobs and earn less money. Still, social class is not marked by any distinctive dialect, and rich people do not live especially extravagant lifestyles.

One detail that gives Iceland the appearance of a relatively classless society lies in the system of personal naming. Iceland retains the medieval practice of using only a single personal name, with further identification provided by a patronymic, which is the name of one's father (or in some instances, one's mother) followed by the suffix "-son" if he is male and "-dóttir" if she is female.

This means that all people have the same form of address in both formal and informal circumstances, unlike the range of clues about status that is conveyed by the choice of name form to address someone in the United States or elsewhere.

In Iceland, literally everyone is addressed by their first name. There are only two exceptions where titles are used: the president and the bishop of Iceland. The spirit of egalitarianism is enshrined in the Icelandic Constitution in a clause prohibiting the creation of nobilities.

A SMALL BUT ACTIVE POPULATION

Icelanders are exceptionally well-educated. Literacy is universal. Many Icelanders are also fluent in Danish and English.

As well as being well-educated, Icelanders are very cultured. This is apparent in their strong support of the arts. Reykjavík contains a truly remarkable range of artistic institutions—a ballet troupe, an opera company, a symphony orchestra, two theaters, numerous art galleries—for a town with a population of around 100,000 people. Such a level of cultural activity is only possible because Icelanders are such avid patrons of the arts.

Icelanders stay well abreast of current affairs, both domestic and international. They have a wide range of national newspapers to choose from to keep themselves informed.

The same is true of literature. Iceland has the highest concentration of bookstores per capita in the world. A remarkable number of Icelanders are poets and novelists. Ten percent of them will publish a book in their lifetime!

To keep Icelanders abreast of current affairs, there are five national newspapers published in Reykjavík. The three largest, *Ftettabladid*, *Morning News*, and *DV* have daily circulations of 75,000, 53,000, and 35,000 respectively. This is remarkable for a country of such small size. Almost everybody in Iceland reads at least one newspaper and most families read two. Icelanders tend to be well-informed about international affairs. They also tend to travel abroad widely.

NATIONALISM

Icelanders have a strong sense of nationalism. They are conscious of their small population size, of the tangential place of their island in world affairs, and of the threat of being overwhelmed by the dominant cultures of the United States or Europe. There is a sense of pride about the distinctiveness of their ways and their ability to prosper despite the rigors of climate and geography. They also look proudly on their long heritage of unusual achievement.

Icelandic nationalism is apparent in various international forums. Joining NATO and accepting the U.S. base have been matters of considerable debate because they are seen to threaten a loss of national sovereignty. Despite the economic benefits, the government negotiated in 1994 for a reduction in the U.S. presence. Similarly, Iceland has resisted joining the European Union.

Icelandic nationalism was evident in the expansion of the Icelandic fishing zones. During the cod wars, feelings against Britain ran high. The same attitude is implicit in Icelanders' reluctance to accept the ban on whaling.

TRADITION AND DRESS

Icelanders have a lively sense of tradition. This is fostered by an interest in personal genealogy. The medieval sagas are still popular reading in Iceland today. During a festival like Thorrablót, Icelanders like to sample traditional foods. Similarly, traditional dress is worn by some people on a festival like Independence Day.

Icelanders today dress much like most Americans or Europeans. Indeed, many Icelanders are very fashion conscious. Designer-label clothes sell well in Reykjavík as Icelanders love to dress up on a Friday or Saturday night.

Iceland's most distinctive contribution to fashion lies in knitwear. Icelanders still wear heavy sweaters in traditional designs made from Icelandic wool. These sweaters are traditionally made in white or earth colors with a decorative design around the yoke. They are effective for keeping Icelanders warm despite the cold weather.

Traditional national costumes have been revived by the Reykjavík Folk-Dancing Society and as part of the Independence Day festivities. Women's traditional dress consists of a black skirt of homespun cloth and a black knitted cardigan with a high neckline, long sleeves, and a slight opening above the bust to give a view of the white shirt underneath. Fancy dresses might have used such imported material as linen, velvet, and silk. Such a dress would be completed with a silk neckerchief like a cravat, and a waist belt. Most striking of all is the headwear: either a knitted cap with a tassel or a tall white cascading headdress. The men's traditional dress consists of a dark-colored tunic and breeches tucked into long socks. Men, too, wear cravat-like neckerchiefs and distinctive headgear: long conical woolen caps.

Traditional Icelandic dress consists of a long skirt and a white shirt worn under a vest or cardigan. There are, however, many variations in color, embroidery, and material.

LIFESTYLE

ICELANDERS ARE DEDICATED WORKERS and consumers and have a very strong work ethic. Children as young as 12 begin working during the summer. Many adults hold two jobs. Icelanders work a longer week than people in virtually any other industrialized nation. All this is required to earn money for spending on the good things that Icelanders enjoy in abundance: fashionable clothes, consumer durables, foreign travel, and cultural events.

Environment, too, plays a major if unquantifiable part in forming the national lifestyle. The long dark winters may well encourage the tendency to party and drink, as well as to enjoy music and write. The long days of summer must play some part in explaining Icelanders' intense energy, evident both in their hard work and hard play. The very bleakness of the elements in Iceland may encourage both a sense of self-sufficiency and also a sense of community in defiance of the wind and the rain, the darkness, the volcanoes, and the glaciers.

Left: **Icelanders work hard so that they can enjoy the finer things in life, such as expensive cars.**

Opposite: **A family finds time to picnic by a waterfall, fitting it into a schedule that includes one of the longest work weeks among industrialized countries.**

65

A STRONG SENSE OF SOCIETY

Icelanders live out their lives of intense work and intense play with a strong sense of society. The small size of the population encourages the idea that everybody knows everybody. This sense of community has a positive side to it since it suggests that anybody can become famous, that everyone should try to live to their fullest potential, and that family, friends, and acquaintances will help out in the event of any trouble. This same sense of community also has a flip side. When the latest fad sweeps the country, such as the trend for owning cell phones, Icelanders feel a strong need to keep up with their neighbors and follow the fashion. The sense that everyone knows everyone else's business may encourage Icelandic youth, in particular, to develop a rebellious streak, which may explain the growing drug scene in Reykjavík. For all age groups, the implicit pressures of social conformity may account for the binge drinking that is a common feature of Icelandic life, especially on a Friday night.

HAPPINESS

It is difficult to make comparisons between nationalities with respect to happiness. An international survey conducted in 2005 found that more than 70 percent of Icelanders declared themselves happy. This percentage is more than that of any other nationality in the world. This has been explained as a closing of ranks by a small nation to present a good impression when questioned by outsiders, or the mischievous humor characteristic of residents of one of the bleakest islands in the world, but there may be a grain of truth to it.

Icelanders live in a stark but beautiful setting where they have to struggle against the natural elements of earthquakes and glaciers, rough seas and swollen rivers, cold weather and long periods of darkness. However, there are no problems of pollution, no army, and no tradition of militarism. People work very hard, but in return enjoy a very high standard of living and do not face significant unemployment.

Icelandic society is small and cohesive, which means that it lacks diversity and can seem oppressively normative, but this also helps it to be relatively classless and crimeless. Icelandic culture mythologizes the independent-spirited individual, but Icelanders also value family and community. Perhaps Icelanders have reason to be happy people after all.

BIRTH

Most Icelanders love children, so much so that many are brought into the world without the complication of marriage. Sixty-three percent of Icelandic children born between 1996 and 2000 were born out of wedlock, with over 80 percent of firstborns in this category. However, this did not result in a vast number of one-parent families as many young couples get married after having their first child.

Iceland has exceptionally good health care. The infant mortality rate is one of the lowest in the world. At slightly over 13 live births per 1,000 inhabitants per year, the Icelandic population is growing at a rate of about 0.9 percent per year.

Child-rearing duties fall disproportionately on mothers, in part because fathers are generally working very long hours. Since many mothers also work, day-care centers, which are provided by local authorities, are kept very busy.

With an infant mortality rate of three deaths per 1,000 live births and a birth rate of 14 per 1,000 residents, Iceland is one of the few industrialized countries that does not face the problem of an aging population.

Icelandic school children are taught all the usual subjects like mathematics, science, social studies and literature. In addition, all students are taught Danish and English.

EDUCATION

Education is compulsory from the age of 7 to 15 (grades 1–9), while preschool is available for children at age 5 or 6. Schooling is free and textbooks are provided by the local authority. The standardized curriculum provides a grounding in the various principal subjects. Danish is taught from the fourth grade and English from the sixth grade. Swimming is an obligatory part of the curriculum. Children are not divided by abilities at this level of schooling. This encourages a sense of egalitarianism.

Students partake in a range of sports, with handball and soccer being the two most popular. Horseback riding is popular with both boys and girls. Chess and bridge are also popular among students. The easy access to swimming pools heated by geothermal energy makes swimming popular among most young people.

In addition to schooling, Icelandic children are acculturated to many of the attitudes prevailing in society. Girls, in particular, begin entering beauty pageants as young teenagers. All schools have long summer breaks, during which it is normal for Icelandic children to work to earn money. From age 12 or even younger, the local authorities employ youngsters to tidy sidewalks and engage in similar civic duties.

Youngsters typically use the money they earn to buy various luxury items: compact discs, musical instruments, fashionable clothes, or to go out for a night in town. Alternatively, they may start saving up for what

they will want when they are older—such as a car or the down payment on a house.

At the end of the ninth grade, a standardized test, along with the school's record of assessment, is used to select what institution a young Icelander should go to next. Students may go on to secondary or comprehensive school for four years (ages 16 to 19) or to vocational school. Some leave school altogether at 16. These people will typically fill the less-skilled jobs and end up making less money than their peers.

Iceland has five universities: the University of Iceland in Reykjavík, the University of Akureyri, the Iceland University of Education, the Reykjavík University, and the Technical College of Iceland. They are all state-funded and tuition is free. About 1,500 students register at the University of Iceland every year, a figure which represents one-third of the 20-year-olds in Iceland. Most students continue living with their parents during their undergraduate studies, in view of the high price of housing in Reykjavík.

Preschoolers having some fun in the snow. Icelandic children benefit from free education all the way through college.

WORK FOR YOUTHS

After the age of 16, it is common for Icelandic students to hold down a part-time job in addition to continuing their schooling. Jobs such as serving in cafés or helping out in stores are characteristically filled by young people. Other possible jobs include labor-intensive social services, such as looking after the elderly and the disabled. In addition to this part-time work, these students also take temporary jobs in the summer—supervising the younger children employed by the city to tidy up sidewalks or helping to beautify parks, for example.

Much of the money earned by students at this stage is spent on socializing. There are many garage bands playing rock music that have a local following. The major focus of the social scene, however, is

A young man works at the ancient Icelandic craft of boatbuilding.

downtown Reykjavík on a Friday night. For this occasion, young people dress up in their most fashionable clothes and hit the town to see and be seen, partying into the wee hours of the morning.

ICELAND'S TEENAGERS

Young people of both genders go out to party in Reykjavík on Friday nights. Either gender may ask the other for a dance, but boys are more likely to ask girls out for a date than the other way around. Teens spend considerable time on the streets, socializing as they move between locations. Those with access to a car may spend the evening cruising. There

Groups of teenagers wandering the streets are a common sight on Friday or Saturday nights in Reykjavík.

is one fashionable circuit of roads, which is a permanent but happy traffic jam on Friday or Saturday nights, and which even has its own name, the *runtur* (ROON-tohr). At 3 A.M. on the weekends, the streets of downtown Reykjavík are awash in euphoric youngsters hanging out together.

Icelandic teenagers tend to be very busy. In addition to schoolwork, working for money, and socializing on Friday nights, they also tend to lead a full social life during the week. Other activities might center around music (classical or rock) or sports. In addition to doing things with the family, older teenagers might go camping and hiking in the interior with friends for a weekend. Girls are more likely to take part in beauty pageants than boys, while boys are more likely to take up soccer or wrestling.

71

Over 80 percent of Icelandic women work as wage earners outside the home, as do these two radio newscasters.

THE ROLE OF WOMEN

In the past, an Icelandic child might be surprised by the election of male presidents as women in Iceland play a more prominent and more equal role than in many Western countries. There are still, however, some glaring inequalities in opportunities for the sexes. On the average, Icelandic women are paid less than men. They generally occupy less prestigious positions in the workplace, characteristically working in clerical and secretarial jobs.

Despite the presence since 1980 to 1996 of a woman president, no prime minister has been a woman and only 30 percent of deputies in the Althing are women. The accessibility of top jobs seems to be gradually improving, though. The chief justice of the Supreme Court is a woman and four of the 12 cabinet ministers are currently women.

Within the home, Icelandic women bear a disproportionate burden of dosmetic work. Women are more likely to cook the meals for a family and to bear primary responsibility for looking after the children.

The role of women

Icelandic women have organized an effective political force to improve their lot. *Kvennalista*, or the Women's Alliance, was the only political party in the world made up only of women and devoted solely to women's issues to have members elected to a national parliament. In 1975, Icelandic women marked the beginning of the United Nations' Women's Decade by going on a one-day strike, which was repeated at the end of the decade in 1985. Such actions reveal a healthy awareness of the remaining problems of imbalance of opportunity for women and a continuing attempt to deal with the problems. Although the *Kvennalista* disbanded in 1999, its remaining members have since formed the Alliance coalition.

Although women play a more equal role in Iceland than in almost any other Western country, certain traditional attitudes toward the division of work between the sexes still hold sway, as seen in the fact that the burden of child-care still falls disproportionately on women.

MARRIAGE

Most Icelandic couples go through a church wedding after having lived together for a few years. Some even have their first child before they get married.

Marriage went out of fashion in Iceland during the 1960s and 1970s, but has made something of a comeback in recent decades. There is still no stigma on bearing a child out of wedlock. Many Icelandic couples do not get married until they can afford their own house or apartment. Those who go on to university do not graduate until they are at least 24 years old. Young couples in their early 20s often live together with one set of parents. They may choose to have their first child, even though they may have no plans to get married yet. That way they can draw on their parents for advice and support and to act as babysitters.

In the late 1990s, over 80 percent of firstborn children were born out of wedlock. The most illustrious example of an unmarried mother is Vigdís Finnbogadóttir, the former president of Iceland, whose reputation did not suffer because she brought up her daughter, Ástrídur, without marrying.

The actual wedding ceremony of Icelanders is similar to that in the United States, with church weddings common. If the couple already has children, they are incorporated into the ceremony as flower-bearers or similar assistants. A honeymoon abroad is an attractive prospect but is sufficiently expensive that many young couples often have to delay it until they are fully established at work.

FAMILY LIFE

Over 80 percent of Icelanders own and live in their own home, either in a house or in an apartment. Houses are generally made of concrete and often painted in cheerful bright colors. The suburbs around Reykjavík contain many large houses. Here affluent Icelandic families enjoy their well-equipped homes, watch imported movies on their VCR, and park their well-polished family car inside the garage, when they are not out working at their jobs or actively socializing.

Icelandic adults lead lifestyles every bit as hectic as their teenage children. A survey on family values found that Icelanders rate their family as more important than their social life, their possessions, or their work. Fulfilling all four values makes Icelanders a busy people. This hectic lifestyle explains one common besetting sin of Icelandic people: they seem to be always late for appointments.

Most Icelanders own their homes. Those who own houses paint them in bright colors and take pride in their gardens.

THE WORK WEEK

The average workweek in Iceland is 42–49 hours, easily the longest in Europe, and many Icelanders put in further overtime. Some even take on a second job. However, Icelanders also tend to get more vacation time compared to many other nations.

Generally both the man and the woman in a household work outside the home, although the man often works longer hours. Icelanders on the whole are very responsible about work: they tend to take it seriously and both expect and are expected to work hard. Indeed, during the British occupation of World War II, Icelanders looked down on working for the British because such work was considered too easy, with too short a workday and too little commitment required.

Working hours vary for different jobs. Office workers might work from 9 A.M. to 6 P.M. Mondays to Fridays. Some people return home for lunch, others eat in one of Reykjavík's cafés. A second job might occupy evenings or weekends.

Parking wardens work long hours like Icelanders in other jobs, but have to contend with the added element of the weather.

ENTERTAINMENT

When not working, Icelandic adults are active cultural consumers. The success of concerts, plays, and art exhibitions in Reykjavík is premised upon a large proportion of the population of the city turning out to see the latest cultural event, and that expectation is generally fulfilled. Icelanders also read widely, eagerly perusing newly-published books, not to mention the five national newspapers.

Television is, of course, the easiest option for an evening's entertainment. However, Icelanders vegetate in front of the television far less than people in most other nations, including the United States. Until a decade ago,

A family enjoys a horse-
back riding adventure on
the weekend.

television did not broadcast on Thursdays to encourage Icelanders to take part in other social activities.

In addition to cultural events, Icelandic adults socialize in the city, as do their teenage children. Eating dinner out is not much of an Icelandic tradition, inhibited in part by the prohibitive cost. However, adults may visit the bars and discos. There are also numerous movie theaters, which are well frequented.

Icelanders follow sports avidly and participate in sporting activities in the evenings and on weekends. One popular activity in Reykjavík is aerobics, and people often work out three or four times a week. On the weekend, Icelandic families might head off to the interior to go riding or for a camping trip, while in the winter they might go skiing. Both during the week and on the weekend, swimming is an always-popular activity. The well-heated outside pools are tempting in any weather and provide an opportunity for healthy exercise.

A young Icelander dis-embarking from a ferry, returning from a shop-ping trip to Glasgow, Scotland.

TRAVEL

Foreign travel is very expensive but popular among Icelanders. Young Icelanders in their 20s often travel abroad for a long stretch of time, either to earn an advanced degree at a foreign university or simply to broaden their horizons. Shopping trips abroad are popular, too, especially as most consumer goods are considerably cheaper abroad than in Iceland. Glasgow, Scotland, is one of the favorite destinations for Icelanders although Nova Scotia is fast gaining popularity. Icelandair flies Icelanders to these destinations three times a week and these shoppers spend as much as $2,600 each time.

LIFE SPAN

Iceland vies with Japan for the longest life expectancy in the world. Their healthy diet (based on fish), the excellent health care system that is available to everyone, and the tradition of healthy exercise give Icelandic women an average life expectancy of 82.7 years and men a life expectancy of 79.2 years.

When a death occurs, the customs are much the same in Iceland as in the United States and the body is buried or cremated. But death in Iceland is much more visible than in the United States. The attitude of Icelanders toward death reflects once again the small population of the island and the consequent feeling that everybody knows almost everybody else. With a small population, it is very likely that an Icelander will know the person who has died or a bereaved family member. The death of younger people is particularly talked about among Icelanders. If somebody, like a young man, commits suicide during the long winter months, there is considerable interest in and discussion of the event by the whole community.

Practically every Icelander's obituary will be in one of the daily newspapers. These pages are closely scrutinized, particularly by the older generation, who are keenly interested to learn the fate of people they once knew. Similarly, funerals are routinely announced on the radio, and this is regular listening for many older people.

Death is a much more personal affair in Iceland because of the small size of the population, which increases the chances that one will know the deceased or the deceased's family.

RELIGION

NINETY-FIVE PERCENT of Icelanders are Lutheran. The constitution recognizes the Evangelical-Lutheran Church as the state church. However, the constitution guarantees freedom of worship for any faith.

A portion of the taxes Icelanders pay goes to support the activities of the church. Those who do not want to support the church can opt to have their payments support the University of Iceland instead. Eighty-five percent of Icelanders belong to the Church of Iceland. A minority identifies with the Seventh-Day Adventists, the Catholic Church, or a rival Lutheran sect. A small group professes pagan beliefs. Immigration in the past decade has also given rise to small Muslim, Jewish, and Buddhist communities.

Despite the large membership in the established church, religion does not play a particularly noticeable part in most people's daily lives. A strikingly high number of people profess belief in such folk traditions as ghosts and trolls.

Left: **Some of Iceland's churches, like this one, are set against breathtaking backdrops of glaciers and mountains.**

Opposite: **With its towering basalt columns, Akureyri's Lutheran church (Akureyrarkirja) typifies modern church design in Iceland.**

PAGANISM

The ancient pre-Christian religion is unusually well-entrenched in Iceland and has been revived by a small group of modern pagans. Local chieftains acted as pagan priests in early times. (*Right:* A modern pagan priest pours libation at the feet of Thor, god of thunder.) Pagans believed in an extensive pantheon of gods and seem to have also practiced various forms of animism. The gods existed in a parallel world surrounded by such other races as giants and dwarves. Their cosmos was kept together by Yggdrassil, the World Ash Tree—the Old Norse version of the cosmic tree.

Odin (*pictured opposite*) is the chief god of Norse mythology. He is the god of poetry, of wisdom, and of war. He became god of poetry by stealing the mead of poetry from the dwarves. He acquired wisdom by sacrificing his eye at the well of wisdom and by hanging himself on the cosmic tree for three days. Warriors who dedicated themselves to Odin could induce in themselves a war frenzy in which they entered an altered state. In this frenzied state they could feel no pain, which made them very effective as warriors. Such warriors were known as *berserkir* (BAIR-zerh-kaihr), from which we get the English word *berserk*.

Thor is the most single-minded of the gods. He lacks the intellectual side of Odin but generally succeeds in what he sets out to achieve through brute force. His strength is associated with his hammer and is manifested in his creation of thunder. Many Old Icelandic personal names included the word Thor, suggesting that he was worshipped particularly widely in Iceland.

Frey and his sister Freyja are important fertility gods. They are responsible for the productivity of crops and the fertility of animals and humans.

Loki is part god, part giant. He is the trickster god, sometimes playing friendly practical jokes, sometimes thoroughly mean ones. Perhaps his worst deed was his responsibility for the death of Baldur.

Baldur was the son of Odin. He was so beloved by everyone that all of creation agreed that it would not hurt him. Since this was the case, the gods would throw things at him at parties, marveling at how nothing ever hurt him. This galled Loki, who went around creation trying to find any object that had not taken part in the pledge not to hurt Baldur. He finally found that the humble mistletoe had not taken part in the vow. He took a piece of mistletoe, used his magic to

make it into a dart, and gave it to Baldur's blind half-brother, Hodd, to throw at Baldur when the gods were having their fun. Everyone was devastated with grief when the mistletoe pierced Baldur and killed him. Loki was eventually punished for this deed. This is the origin of the tradition of people kissing beneath the mistletoe, making a gesture of peace to atone for its misdeed in killing Baldur.

These gods do not appear particularly moral. Odin sleeps with many different women. He even cheats in his role of selector of the slain in battle. He sometimes unfairly makes the best warrior lose and die so that he can enjoy his company in Valhalla. Unlike the Greek and Roman gods, the Norse gods were mortal, finally dying at Ragnarok (the doom of the gods) in a pitched battle with their enemies. The fact that the gods lost this final battle may explain some of the traditional bleakness of Old Norse culture. At this stage, Baldur comes back to life and the younger generation of gods takes over.

The Roman Catholic cathedral in Reykjavík, pictured at midnight in July. Fewer than 2 percent of Icelanders who identify themselves as Christian are Roman Catholic.

THE CONVERSION

When the first settlers arrived in Iceland, pagan beliefs predominated, although there was religious tolerance even then. It is recorded of one early settler, Helgi the Lean, for example, that he "believed in Christ, and yet made vows to Thor for sea-voyages and in tight corners." The conversion to Christianity occurred in the year 1000, when Thorgeir the lawspeaker accepted Christianity at the Althing for the whole nation, while guaranteeing religious freedom for people who wished to keep pagan ways in private.

This was in part to please the main trading partner for medieval Iceland, the Christianized kings of Norway, and also in part to satisfy the growing Christian faction in Iceland. This relatively late and peaceful adoption of Christianity was important for the retention in Iceland of a fuller record of heathen practices than anywhere else in Europe where heathenism was banished.

LUTHERANISM

The National Church of Iceland, formally called the Evangelical-Lutheran Church, is the state religion, and the president of Iceland is its supreme authority. In religious matters, the bishop of Iceland has ecclesial authority. Karl Sigurbjörnsson is the current bishop of Iceland. The church has about 300 congregations, grouped into 15 district assemblies.

Lutheranism draws on the Reformation preaching of Martin Luther and emphasizes an individual's access to the Scriptures and the importance of individual faith. The major sacraments are baptism and the Eucharist, which are public confirmations of an individual's faith.

Although 85 percent of the population is registered as some form of Lutheran, these statistics are considered rather misleading by some as most Icelandic are automatically registered as members of the state religion. Estimates indicate that only 10 percent of the population attends religious services regularly and that 43 percent do not attend at all.

Many Lutheran churches in Iceland are small simple structures, like this church at Thingvellir. Built in 1859, the Thingvellir Church is one of the best-known churches in Iceland and a tourist attraction.

The Thingvellir Lutheran church.

The altar of a simple church, where the faithful participate in the ritual of the Eucharist.

DAYS OF THE WEEK

Many of the English names for the days of the week are derived from a period in Anglo-Saxon England when people worshiped the same pagan gods that made up the Norse pantheon. Thus, Tuesday is the day of Tyw, a minor god who gives up his hand as a pledge to the wolf Fenrir. Wednesday is the day of Woden, an English spelling for Odin. Thursday is the day of Thor. Friday is the day of Frey. Saturday is the only day named after a Roman god, Saturn. Sunday and Monday take their names from the sun and moon, probably objects of worship in pagan belief. Presumably these names were all so well-established by the time missionaries converted England to Christianity that they were kept despite their pagan overtones.

ICELANDIC NAMES FOR THE DAYS OF THE WEEK

Days	Icelandic name	Meaning
Monday	mánudagur	moon day
Tuesday	þriðudagur	third day
Wednesday	miðvikudagur	middle of the week
Thursday	fimmtudagur	fifth day
Friday	föstudagur	fasting day
Saturday	laugardagur	washing day
Sunday	sunnudagur	sun day

GLÁMUR THE GHOST

One of the most famous ghosts is the spirit of Glámur in *Grettir's Saga*. Glámur, a strong and antisocial shepherd, is killed on Christmas Eve by a ghost near Vatnsdal and is not buried in sanctified ground. As a result, his spirit takes to haunting the farm, including riding on the housetops. He kills the shepherd who replaces him the next Christmas, and generally terrorizes the farmers and their families. Finally the strong man Grettir, hero of the saga, undertakes to help the farmers by challenging the ghost, Glámur, to a duel. The ghost kills Grettir's horse and Grettir waits for a nighttime encounter with Glámur.

When about a third of the night has passed, Grettir hears a loud noise. Something is climbing up the building, riding the roof and kicking with its heels until the timber beams crack. This goes on for some time, and then the thing comes down toward the door. The door opens and Grettir sees Glámur's enormously big and ugly head looming in the door. Glámur moves slowly in, and on passing the door stands upright, reaching to the roof. He turns toward the hall, resting his arms on the crossbeam and peering into the room.

Glámur and Grettir then engage in a mighty wrestling match, destroying much of the hall in the process. At first, Grettir tries to prevent Glámur from dragging him outside, then suddenly overpowers him by switching tactics and pushing him out the door.

Glámur falls head over heels out of the house and Grettir falls on top of him. The moon is shining very brightly outside, with light clouds passing over it and hiding it now and again. At the moment when Glámur falls, the moon shines forth, and Glámur turns his eyes up toward it. Grettir himself relates that that sight is the only one that ever made him tremble. With the fatigue, the loss of his horse, and all else that he has endured, when he sees the horrible rolling of Glámur's eyes, Grettir's heart sinks so utterly that he has no strength to draw his sword, but lies there between life and death. Glámur possesses more malignant power than most fiends, for he now speaks this way:

"You have expended much energy, Grettir, in your search for me. Nor is it to be wondered at that you should have little joy thereof. And now I tell you that you shall possess only half the strength and firmness of heart that were decreed to you if you had not striven with me. And this I lay upon you, that these eyes of mine shall be ever before your vision. You will find it hard to live alone, and at last it shall drag you to death."

When the specter finishes speaking, the faintness that had come over Grettir leaves him. He draws his short sword, cuts off Glámur's head, and lays it between his thighs. Thorhall the farmer praises God and thanks Grettir warmly for having laid to rest this unclean spirit. Then they set to work and burn Glámur to cold cinders, bind the ashes in a skin, and bury them in a place far away from the haunts of man or beast.

After this incident, Grettir, the great strong man and outlaw, is afraid to be alone in the dark.

Odd-shaped rocks such as this one were explained by early Icelanders as trolls who did not leave themselves enough time to get back to their homes in the earth before sunrise.

FOLK BELIEFS

A survey on attitudes toward the supernatural in Western Europe found that the majority of Icelanders claim to believe in, or at least do not deny the existence of elves. Over 40 percent of Icelanders claimed some kind of contact with the dead, as opposed to an average of 20 percent in Western Europe.

ELVES are generally friendly creatures of the Otherworld. They are human in form, very beautiful, and only appear when they choose to. Legend has it that they are descended from the children of Eve whom Eve hid from God because she had not washed them. Thus, God decreed that they should be Hidden People for all time. Icelanders make allowances for the elf world. The main street of Grundarfjördur has houses on one side with consecutive even numbers except for a jump from 82 to 86. Between these two houses there is a large rock: The elves are believed to live at No. 84.

TROLLS are large, elemental, and generally malevolent beings. The most famous troll is probably Gryla, the giant troll woman of the mountains whose sons are the more friendly, if still mischievous, 13 Father Christmases of Icelandic tradition. Gryla herself is a mean old troll, invoked by parents with naughty children for her habit of eating children who misbehave.

Trolls have to return to their homes in the earth before daylight or they will be turned into stone. Many large stones in the Icelandic countryside are explained as the figures of trolls who stayed out too long, including Hvítserkur, a stone troll cow, caught by the sun drinking seawater off the northwest coast of Iceland.

GHOSTS in the form of the spirits of dead people are much more corporeal in Iceland than in the usual Western tradition. Such spirits sometimes made their fun in the olden days by riding a house at night, sitting on top of the roof and making a lot of noise as they whipped the house into action with their heels, as does the ghost Glámur in *Grettir's Saga*. Of course, since traditional old houses had roofs covered in grass, and since there were plenty of sheep and other animals around that might choose to feed on that grass, there may be a more rational explanation for these "riding" noises.

The open attitude of Icelanders to the supernatural discovered in the survey is explained by Icelandic psychologist Dr. Arni Björnsson: "Most of us do not actively believe in these things, but on the other hand, we are reluctant to deny their existence. It is really a form of skepticism. We live in a land which is highly unpredictable—what is grass and meadow today could be lava and ash tomorrow. So we have learned not to rely too much on the factual evidence of our senses."

"Iceland is a big country for such a small population. We've plenty of room for neighbors of all kinds."
–Icelandic psychologist Dr. Arni Björnsson

LANGUAGE

THE ICELANDIC LANGUAGE is a cousin to the English language. The far-distant origins of both languages lie in an old Germanic language shared both by the Angles and Saxons who later migrated to England and by the predecessors of the Viking Norwegians who later migrated to Iceland.

The different languages have, of course, developed in rather different ways. Icelandic is a strikingly standardized and conservative language. There are almost no dialectal variants between regions in spoken Icelandic, unlike the vast array of dialects of spoken English.

Opposite: **An advertisement in Icelandic at the back of a bus.**

Below: **Signs written in Icelandic. Although Icelandic uses the Romanized alphabet as does English, it also uses a number of accents and has a couple of special characters not found in English.**

THE CONTINUITY OF ICELANDIC

English has changed considerably in the last 1,000 years. As the Anglo-Saxons suffered conquest by the Normans, rediscovered Greek and Latin culture, and explored the New World, their language was influenced by these encounters. Icelandic, on the other hand, changed little over this time. Modern Icelandic is quite close to Old Icelandic. The language of the medieval sagas is as easy for today's Icelanders to read as the language of Shakespeare is for contemporary English speakers, in contrast with the obscurity of the language of *Beowulf*, with which it is more contemporary.

The English language accepts words from other languages very readily. Words like *burrito* and *potato* are taken from another language to describe a concept or object new to English. Such borrowings are known as loan words. English also borrows readily from Greek and Latin to explain new concepts, such as *telephone*, which is made up of the Greek words for "far" and "sound," or *television*, made up from the Greek word for "far" and the Latin word for "seeing."

Icelandic is very resistant to such borrowings. A form of the word *telephone* has been absorbed into most languages (German *telefon*, French *téléphone*, Italian *telefono*). The Icelandic word is *sími* (SEE-mi), which is an adaptation of a native word for a length of thread. Likewise, Icelanders resist using the term *computer*, which is called *tölva* (TEHL-vah) *(see below)*, a blend of the Icelandic words *tala* (TAO-lah), meaning "number," and *völva* (VEHL-vah), meaning "prophetess."

One standard method of word formation in Icelandic is by combining existing words (such as *birdbath* in English). The resulting compound words can be rather a mouthful. For example, the treasury is called *fjármálaráduneyti* (FYAHR-mahl-rah-thoh-NAY-ti; where *fjár* = money, *mál* = matter, affairs, *ráð* = plan or authority, *ráduneyti* = a department); an idealist is a *hugsjónamadur* (HOHGS-yoon-nah-MAH-thor; where *hugsun* = thought, *sjón* = vision, *madur* = person); and a rebel is an *uppreisnarmadur* (OHP-prize-nahr-MAH-thor; an uprising person).

Although modern English is substantially different from Old English, as can be seen from the excerpt from Beowulf *(below)*, Old Icelandic manuscripts *(left)* can be easily read by today's Icelanders.

THE ICELANDIC ALPHABET

Icelandic has a number of letters in addition to those in the English alphabet. Þ and þ known as thorn (replaced by *th* throughout this book), represents the sound of the English *th* in a word like *thin*. Ð and T, known as eð (replaced by *d* in this book) represents the sound of the English *th* in a word like *then*. The other additions are to the vowels. Icelandic has a differentiated set of long vowels, which are spelled with an accent, as in í. Icelandic also has the vowels ö and æ, which represent the sounds of the vowel in the English words turn and eye.

The letter þ derives from an earlier form of script, known as the runic alphabet, which was used for inscriptions in Old Icelandic. This same script was also occasionally used in Old English for inscriptions and throughout Northern Europe in medieval times.

3005 æfter hæleða hryre,   hwate scildwigan,
    folcrēd fremede,   oððe furður gēn
    eorlscipe efnde. —   Nū is ofǫst betost,
    þæt wē þēodcyning   þǣr scēawian,
    ond þone gebringan,   þē ūs bēagas geaf,
3010 on ādfære.   Ne scel ānes hwæt
    meltan mid þām mōdigan,   ac þǣr is māðma hord,
    gold unrīme   grimme gecēa(po)d,
    ond nū æt sīðestan   sylfes fēore
    bēagas (geboh)te;   þā sceall brond fretan,
3015 ǣled þeccean, —   nalles eorl wegan
    māððum tō gemyndum,   nē mægð scȳne
    habban on healse   hringweorðunge,
    ac sceal geōmormōd,   golde berēafod
    oft nalles ǣne   elland tredan,
3020 nū se herewīsa   hleahtor ālegde,
    gamen ond glēodrēam.   Forðon sceall gār wesan
    monig morgenceald   mundum bewunden,
    hæfen on handa,   nalles hearpan swēg

Anna P. Salvarsdóttir	kvensjúkdómar og fæðingarhjálp
Arnar Hauksson dr. med.	kvensjúkdómar og fæðingarhjálp
Benedikt Ó. Sveinsson	kvenlækningar, kvenkrabbameinslækningar
Björn Árdal	barnalækningar, ónæmis- og ofnæmisfræði
Einar Sindrason	háls-, nef- og eyrnalækningar
Ellen Mooney	húðsjúkdómar og húðmeinafræði
Friðrik P. Jónsson	háls-, nef-og eyrnalækningar
Grétar Sigurbergsson	geðlækningar
Guðjón Haraldssoi	alm. skurðlækningar og þvagfæraskurðlækningar
Gunnar H. Gunnlaugsson	alm. skurðlækningar, brjóstholsskurðl.
Kjartan J. Kjartansson	geðlækningar
Konráð Sigurðsson	heimilislækningar
Kristófer Þorleifsson	geðlækningar
Magnús E. Kolbeinsson	skurðlækningar
Ólafur M. Hakansson	kvensjúkdómar og fæðingarhjálp
Ósk Ingvarsdóttir	kvensjúkdómar og fæðingarhjálp
Ragnar Arinbjarnar	heimilislækningar
Ragnar Finnsson	svæfingar og deyfingar
Sigurður Ólafsson	lyflækningar og meltingarsjúkdómar
Sigurveig Þ. Sigurðardóttir	barnalækningar, ónæmis- og ofnæmisfræði

This listing of doctors shows the prevalence of the patronymic system in Iceland.

THE NAMING SYSTEM

Surnames or family names came into English gradually over the course of the last thousand years. The system of naming that evolved is similar in most countries. Iceland, however, retains an older system where everybody has only one name, a first name. In order to distinguish individuals with the same name, a patronymic is added.

For example, Gudrún Erlendsdóttir, the Chief Justice of the Supreme Court, is called Gudrún in both informal and formal circumstances. Her second name, or patronymic, is simply the name of her father, Erlendur, with the suffix *-dóttir*, meaning daughter. Her own daughter might be called Sigrún Gudrúnsdóttir. Boys and men make their patronymic through the suffix *-son*, as in Jón Sigurdsson, who would generally be called Jón and whose father was Sigurd. His own son might be called Magnús Jónsson.

One consequence of this system is that grandparents are not connected to their grandchildren by name. Magnús Jónsson's son might be called Páll Magnússon, which gives no clue that his grandfather was Jón Sigurdsson. Another consequence is that there is no question of a woman changing her name when she gets married. The system does, however, still contain some inequalities in the treatment of gender. Patronymics for both boys and girls are generally drawn from the father's name. The mother's name is used as the root only when there is no father.

In the Icelandic telephone directory, everyone is listed and the entries are alphabetized by first name. It is proper to refer to everybody by that name except for two dignitaries who are addressed by their title: the president and the bishop of Iceland.

There is a fossil of this system of patronymics in English family names, as in the name "Johnson." Clearly, this only applies to a small group of family names in English, whereas in Iceland it is almost universal. There was a period in the 1940s when Western European-style family names became popular. This explains the name of the famous Icelandic novelist Halldór Laxness, who chose to adopt a place name as his family name. The system of patronymics is currently very strong, however. Ninety percent of Icelanders use the system of patronymics, and it is no longer legal to switch to family names. Indeed, any foreigner who adopts Icelandic citizenship also has to adopt a suitable patronymic.

THE RUNIC ALPHABET

Runes are an early form of lettering used for inscriptions and magic signs throughout Northern Europe in the Middle Ages. The script was first devised for writing on wood, which is why it is formed of straight lines and why there are no lines perpendicular to the uprights—they would get lost in the grain of the wood. Runic script is also known as *futhark* after its first six letters.

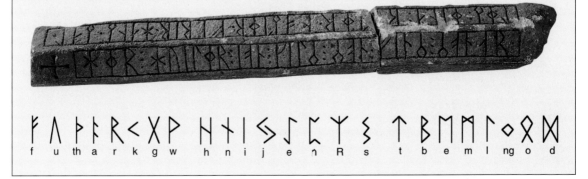

ARTS

LITERATURE HAS BEEN ICELAND'S most outstanding contribution to the world of arts. The country is most famous for its sagas, tales of heroes and kings of the 12th to 14th centuries. The richness of this early literature may be connected to the Icelandic environment: long and dark winter nights before the invention of electric lighting gave early Icelanders ample opportunity for storytelling, while Iceland's sheep provided parchment on which to write those tales. (Parchment is made from thin sheep or goat skin.) Whatever the reason, Iceland has one of the most notable literary traditions of the Middle Ages, and the country continues to have a significant literary production.

Opposite: **Visitors admiring some contemporary sculptures in Reykjavík's national museum. Arts and literature thrive in Iceland.**

Below: **Many modern sculptures like this can be seen around Reykjavík.**

MEDIEVAL LITERATURE

Iceland has a richness of medieval prose literature unparalleled in the rest of medieval Europe. The family sagas are in some ways like novels. They revolve around conflicts between families and questions of loyalty and revenge, unfolding in a realistic setting in the stark beauty of medieval Iceland.

A striking range of Old Icelandic poetry also survives. There are two poetic traditions. One is derived from an extensive collection of mythological and heroic verse known as *The Elder Edda*. The other is a tradition of extremely complex praise poetry, with many musical effects such as alliteration, rhyme, half-rhyme, and assonance. This latter kind is known as skaldic verse after the Icelandic name for the poets, skalds, (SKAHLDS) who recited it.

Not all the mythological poetry is austere and serious. One poem tells of the predicament faced by the gods when the giant Thrym steals Thor's hammer, which is the source of his strength. Thrym demands to be married to Freyja before he will return the hammer. Freyja absolutely refuses such a suggestion, disdaining the stain on her reputation. The gods meet in council and decide that the only solution is to send Thor in a woman's dress, pretending that he is Freyja. Loki accompanies him, dressed as his bridesmaid.

When the two gods get to the wedding feast, Thrym is surprised and perhaps appalled at the vast appetite of his wife-to-be, who devours huge portions with no ladylike manners. Loki explains that "Freyja" has been fasting while waiting for the marriage and so is ravenously hungry. Thrym is apparently contented with this answer. Next he lifts up his betrothed's veil to steal a kiss, but leaps back when he sees such fiery red eyes. Loki explains again, claiming that "Freyja" has not slept for nights in excited anticipation of the wedding. Finally, Thrym's sister asks what present she is going to get at the wedding. At this point, Thor's hammer is produced to hallow the wedding ceremonies. Thor grabs it and kills all the giants present. Thrym's sister gets a blow from the hammer as her wedding gift.

Icelandic skalds were particularly successful at their task of praising kings. Iceland provided court poets throughout much of Europe, chronicling in particular the acts of Norway's kings. These poets acted rather like the journalists of their day, spreading the reputation of deserving (or well-paying) kings and lords in glowing verses.

Looking at an illustrated manuscript of the *Eddas*, which form the most authoritative source for ancient Norse mythology.

NJÁLL'S SAGA

Probably the most famous medieval Icelandic family saga is *Njáll's Saga*. This gripping saga tells of the friendship between the lawyer and promoter of peace, Njáll, and the more classic hero Gunnarr. While Njáll acts as a lawyer and arranger of affairs in Iceland, Gunnarr sails to Denmark and Norway, winning fame with the king there. On his return, Gunnarr marries the impetuous and long-haired beauty, Hallgerd, who has already caused the death of two previous husbands. Hallgerd quarrels with Njáll's wife, Bergthóra, in a dispute that develops into a feud, but Njáll and Gunnarr keep reconciling after the resulting killings and remain friends.

Meanwhile, the dark figure of Mörd incites the friends Otkell and Skammkell into a feud with Gunnarr by convincing Hallgerd to steal provisions from Otkell. When Gunnarr discovers that Hallgerd has organized the theft of provisions from Otkell, he is so furious that he loses his temper and slaps Hallgerd. She vows to herself and to Gunnarr that she will one day avenge this blow, which later leads to grave consequences.

Gunnarr offers monetary compensation to Otkell for the theft of his provisions, but the offer is refused and the feud continues to escalate despite Gunnarr's best attempts at restraint. Njáll advises his friend that he will only survive the feud if he will, at all costs, avoid killing more than once in the same family.

When the mischief-maker Mörd learns of Njáll's prophecy to Gunnarr, he deliberately arranges things so that Gunnarr cannot avoid killing two members of the same family. A legal case at the local *thing* is brought against Gunnarr, who is outlawed for three years. As he sets out to leave Iceland, however, his horse stumbles and he slips from the saddle and looks up to the slopes of his farm:

"How lovely the slopes are," he says, "more lovely than they have ever seemed to me before—golden cornfields and new-mown hay. I am going back home, and I will not go away."

Gunnarr's enemies gather and attack him when he is alone in his farmhouse with his wife and mother. He defends himself nobly until one of the attackers manages to cut through the bowstring of his bow.

Gunarr says to Hallgerd, "Let me have two locks of your hair, and help my mother braid them into a bowstring for me."

"Does anything depend on it?" asks Hallgerd.

"My life depends on it," replies Gunnarr, "for my enemies will never overcome me as long as I can use my bow."

"In that case," says Hallgerd, "I shall now remind you of the slap you once gave me, and the vow I made to avenge that blow. I do not care in the least whether you hold out a long time or not."

"To each his own way of earning fame," says Gunnarr. "You shall not be asked again."

Gunnarr is then duly killed.

In the second half of the saga, the evil Mörd precipitates yet another feud, this time between Njáll and Flosi. Both Njáll and Flosi do all they can to avert the feud, but finally cannot help but be drawn into it by the demands of honor and the workings of fate. A major attempt to settle the quarrel at the Althing fails. Flosi gathers a large force around the farm of Njáll and his sons, besieges their home and then sets fire to it. He offers Njáll and Bergthóra, who are by this time an old couple, the chance to escape alive.

"I have no wish to go outside," says Njáll, "for I am an old man now and ill-equipped to avenge my sons; and I do not want to live in shame."

Flosi says to Bergthora, "You come out, Bergthora, for under no circumstances do I want you to burn."

Bergthora staunchly replies, "I was given to Njáll in marriage when young, and I have promised him that we would share the same fate."

Then they both go back inside.

Njáll and his sons all die, but his son-in-law, Kári, manages to escape, which ensures that the feud continues.

Another attempt at reconciling the quarrel at the Althing fails, this time ending in an outright battle at the Althing. Kári single-mindedly exacts vengeance on the killers of his family. Both Flosi and Kári travel abroad, finally going to Rome to seek absolution. Flosi gets back to his farm in Iceland before Kári. During his return in winter, Kári's boat is shipwrecked on the shores of Iceland.

When Kári and his men make it to shore, it is snowing furiously. Kári's plan is to go to Svinafell and put Flosi's nobility to the test. He and his men walk to Svinafell through the snowstorm. On entering, they find Flosi sitting in the main room. He recognizes Kári at once and jumps up to welcome him, embraces him, and places Kári on the high seat beside him. He invites Kári to stay the winter, and Kári accepts. Flosi and Kári make a full reconciliation, and thus the feud ends.

Halldór Laxness, Iceland's Nobel Prize-winning novelist.

MODERN LITERATURE

The most famous modern Icelandic writer by far is Halldór Laxness (1902–98), winner of the Nobel Prize in literature in 1955. He parodied the medieval family sagas in *Gerpla* (1952), in which he satirized the too-ready recourse to violence throughout the ages. Another of his novels, *The Atomic Station*, published in 1948, anticipated the controversy about the U.S. airbase at Keflavík. The novelist was strongly critical of the willingness of Icelandic politicians to give up Iceland's independence. Probably the most famous novel by Halldór Laxness is *Independent People* (1934). Here the novelist promoted the cause of Icelandic independence before the full break from Denmark while not over-glamorizing life in Iceland. He described the gritty and sometimes petty reality of an Icelandic small farmer, while at the same time glorifying that farmer's defiant spirit of independence.

Icelandic literature has continued to thrive since Halldór Laxness. Halldór's novels represent a tradition of social commentary through acute observation of everyday life. Others have written in this tradition, while a non-realist tradition is evident in the modernist works of Thor Vilhjálmsson. His novels have won many literary prizes. Many younger novelists continue to publish interesting work, such as Einar Már Gudmundsson's *Angels of the Universe*, a novel portraying a man's destructive behavior and his subsequent descent into schizophrenia. This work was awarded the Nordic Council's Literature Award in 1995.

Poetry thrives in modern Iceland and is spurred on not just by the high literacy rate but also by a living tradition of memorizing and reciting poetry. Poets played a significant role in Iceland's struggle for independence. Jónas Hallgrímsson (1807–45) is one of the most admired poets of modern Iceland. He pioneered a new movement in poetry and literature, which reshaped the language of poetry and prose, opened the Icelanders' eyes to the beauty of their land, and accelerated their determination to achieve political independence. Halldór Laxness calls him the "poet of Icelandic consciousness."

Jón Sigurdsson, the important 19th-century independence figure, was a poet. In the 20th century, Steinn Steinarr was an important modernist poet who wrote in free verse. A group of poets from the 1950s who broke from traditional forms became known as the "atom poets" for their modern approach. The most popular poet of the postwar generation is Hannes Pétursson, who turned back to old metrical forms to deal with modern themes. All Icelandic poets show a deep sense of historical tradition by either reacting to the past or revisiting it.

Icelandic drama looks back to Matthías Jochumsson's *Útilegumennirnir* (*The Outlaws*, 1862), as the beginning of a tradition blending popular romance with native folktale. The most important modern playwright is Jökull Jakobsson, whose work blends theater of the absurd with realist drama on political themes to search for the meaning of life. Recent work continues the exploration of political and social problems in plays by Kjartan Ragnarsson and others.

This statue memorializes the folktale *The Outlaws*, upon which Matthías Jochumsson's play is based.

A painting by Jóhannes Kjarval.

VISUAL ARTS

There is no very extensive tradition of painting in Iceland. One of the first painters to capture the Icelandic landscape on canvas was Ásgrímur Jónsson (1876–1958). He painted the light on the landscape in watercolors influenced by the Impressionists. His home and studio in Reykjavík have become a museum of his art.

Jóhannes Kjarval (1885–1972) is probably Iceland's most popular painter. He studied briefly in England and was strongly influenced by J.M.W. Turner. His paintings include a range of styles, tending toward the abstract and dreamlike. On his 70th birthday, a retrospective of his work was viewed by 25,000 people, over an eighth of the population of Iceland at the time. On his death, a museum of his works was established in Reykjavík.

Subsequent artists, such as Thorvaldur Skúlason (1906–84), turned from landscapes to an art engaged with Iceland's urban life or the fishing industry and to more abstract art. Most Icelandic artists receive training abroad. Some have made their home abroad, such as the leading figurative painter Louisa Matthíasdóttir (1917–2000) who lived and worked in New York.

Einar Jónsson (1874–1954) was Iceland's first significant sculptor. His early work, "Outlaws," portrays a scene from *The Saga of Gisli* in realistic style. He subsequently combined this style with a private symbolism. His home is now a museum, where his works are kept on display.

There are a large number of contemporary visual artists in Iceland working in a wide range of styles and mediums.

MUSIC

Icelandic youths listen to both U.S. and European pop music and a number also play in garage bands. In 1986 the Icelandic band the Sugarcubes made it to worldwide prominence after they gained an international following in England. Björk Gudmundsdóttir, former lead singer of the Sugarcubes, continues to bring Icelandic pop music to the rest of the world. She has released more than seven albums, most of them critically acclaimed. In May 2000, Björk won the Best Actress award at Cannes for the film *Dancer in the Dark*.

Classical music came late to Iceland. Icelandic music remained essentially medieval into the 19th century. In relatively recent times, the necessary institutions for classical music have all developed on a small scale, with the founding of the Reykjavík Conservatory of Music in 1930, the National Symphony Orchestra in 1950, and a biennial Reykjavík Festival of the Arts since 1970. There are now high quality classical concerts in Reykjavík all summer long.

Björk Gudmundsdóttir swept to international fame as the lead singer for the Sugarcubes. In 1993, Björk left the Sugarcubes for a solo career. Always conscious of her image, she is a favorite model for fashion designer Jean-Paul Gaultier.

Movie director Hrafn Gunnlaugsson *(center)* giving actors directions during the making of a Viking movie.

MOVIES

Since 1980, a fledgling Icelandic movie industry has started making movies that have gained some international recognition. Many of these movies hark back to the Saga Age, and movies that feature Vikings are still popular, both in Iceland and abroad.

Icelandic movie-makers are mainly concerned with Icelandic attitudes, history, and subjects of importance for Icelanders, reflecting pride in their land and traditions. But some have combined Icelandic topics with Western movie-making styles, such as Hrafn Gunnlaugsson's movie, *When the Raven Flies*, which portrays medieval Iceland through the conventions of the spaghetti Western.

Thorsteinn Jónsson's *The Atomic Station*, based on the novel of the same name by Halldór Laxness, was shown at the Cannes Film Festival in 1984.

In 1992 Fridrik Pór Fridriksson's *Children of Nature* was nominated in the Best Foreign Film category at the Academy Awards.

CRAFTS

Icelandic sheep need thick fleece to endure the rigors of the Icelandic winter. The outer layer of coarse wool is naturally waterproof, while the inner layers of fine wool retain warmth close to the skin. The fleece, which is shorn from the sheep in the spring and spun into high-quality wool yarn, forms the basis for the traditional Icelandic handicraft of knitting warm sweaters.

There is a classic design for traditional Icelandic sweaters. The body is generally white or earth-toned, while a geometric pattern at the yoke adds a splash of color and design.

Iceland's international airport at Keflavík is a thriving outlet for Icelandic knitwear. Passengers traveling on Icelandair between the United States and Europe have every opportunity to boost the economy of Iceland by buying an Icelandic sweater even during the shortest of layovers.

Iceland is famous for its distinctively patterned sweaters, knitted from the country's finest wool.

LEISURE

ICELANDERS ARE, ON THE WHOLE, active people who take part in a wide range of sports and games. The population is, however, too small for the country to have much impact on the international sports scene. Still, soccer is pursued with considerable enthusiasm, and Iceland is a force to be reckoned with in international handball tournaments. Other leisure pastimes include both the more cerebral and the more social.

Television programs are mostly imported from Britain and the United States, and they are telecasted with Icelandic subtitles. Until a few years ago, television did not broadcast on Thursday nights. This encouraged Icelanders to be active participants rather than passive viewers. Even with nightly broadcasting, Icelanders have more of a tradition of an actively engaged social life than most other nations.

Left: **Entire families often go horseback riding in the interior.**

Opposite: **Fishing is a popular weekend activity. Here, two men are fishing for trout in Grenlaekur River.**

SPORTS

After soccer, handball is the most popular year-round game since it is played on indoor courts. Iceland ranks among the top 12 nations in the world at this fast-paced game. Basketball is becoming increasingly popular as well.

Boxing is banned in Iceland, but there is a traditional form of Icelandic wrestling known as *glíma* (GLEE-mah), which has been practiced since the early days of settlement in Iceland. Similar in many ways to Japanese sumo wrestling, *glíma* wrestlers wear harnesses on their thighs and hips which their opponent grabs in an attempt to throw them to the ground.

Icelanders do well in international contests in track and in sports relying on strength. Vala Flosadóttir won the 2000 Olympic bronze medal for pole vaulting.

Soccer is extremely popular in Iceland. The game is played by young people everywhere during summer. This is a portrait of an all-girl soccer team in their bright red uniforms.

OUTDOOR ACTIVITIES

Horseback riding was the usual means of land transportation throughout Iceland for centuries. It remains a significant pastime today, offering the opportunity to explore the beauty of the remote parts of the country.

Hiking is a favorite activity for both Icelanders and tourists as this enables them to take in the starkly beautiful scenery of the coast and

ICELANDIC HORSES

Icelandic horses (*right*) are small but sturdy beasts. They are a distinctive breed, descended from horses brought over by the early settlers. No horses have been imported into Iceland for the last 800 years, so that the stock has evolved to best suit local conditions. The resulting horses are remarkably sure-footed at covering the unstable and lava-strewn terrain of the Icelandic countryside.

Icelandic horses are unique for having a distinctive fifth gait. The four gaits usual to all horses are the walk, trot, canter, and gallop. Icelandic horses have a gait between the trot and canter, known as the *tölt* (tehlt), which is faster than a trot but smoother than a canter, with the rider staying secure in the saddle. This makes it ideal for covering long distances at a comfortable pace.

interior. Fishing for salmon and trout is also a popular activity, although fishing licenses can be very expensive. Hunting is popular, particularly of ptarmigan in the fall.

Skiing is a favorite sport and there are some good ski resorts throughout Iceland. Bláfjöll, Iceland's largest ski resort, is located just 30 minutes away from Reykjavík. Cross-country skiing is a popular alternative to hiking in winter. Locals and tourists also take advantage of the outdoor splendors by snowmobiling, ice-climbing, and trekking over glaciers.

Iceland's environment is not ideal for golf due to the lack of smooth areas of earth, the strong winds, and the unpredictable weather. Nevertheless, golf is played at a number of courses throughout Iceland. There is an international tournament called the Arctic Open, which takes advantage of the midnight sun during the summer at Akureyri in the north. In late June a 36-hole international match is held, with tee-off at midnight and play continuing until the early hours of the morning.

Swimming is a popular activity. Small communities have outdoor pools where the water is heated by geothermal energy. As swimming is a compulsory part of the school curriculum, all Icelanders can swim. Many public swimming pools also include a hot tub or jacuzzi of hot water for relaxing in.

MIND GAMES

Chess has a considerable following in Iceland. In 1972 American Bobby Fischer defeated Boris Spassky, the then reigning world champion, in an avidly followed championship match held in Reykjavík.

Iceland has nine grandmasters of chess, a remarkably high number for such a small country. The Icelandic National Chess Championship is a significant contest. In particular, chess has a special association with the tiny island of Grímsey, north of Akureyri, which juts into the Arctic Circle. Grímsey was famed as an island inhabited by chess fanatics from an early time. In the 19th century, this reputation came to the notice of Daniel Willard Fiske, a wealthy U.S. scholar of Old Icelandic who was also a chess champion. Fiske donated 11 marble chess sets to the farmers on the island. The chess sets are still there, although it is no longer true that the Grímsey islanders are chess fanatics.

Bridge is also a popular game among many Icelanders. In 1991 the Icelandic team won the World Bridge Championship held in Japan. The tournament was broadcast live on Icelandic television and watched with rapt attention by most of the population.

FRIDAY NIGHT

On the weekend in Reykjavík, and especially on Friday nights, young people head out for a night on the town. The crowd in their 20s—20 is the legal drinking age—may spend the evening in a bar or at a club. Those under 20 years old also hit the town and are generally more visible in their celebrations. The festivities usually go on very late.

Friday night gives Icelandic youths an opportunity to dress up in the latest fashions. Typically, a group of friends will congregate at someone's house at about 9 P.M. for some conversation before heading downtown. Around midnight, the group goes to the bars or clubs downtown, meet other friends, and generally see what is happening and be seen. It is unfashionable to turn up before midnight. Those with access to cars—17 is the minimum age for getting a license—cruise in a fashion-conscious traffic jam known as *runtur*, a circuit of the downtown streets that is the place to be on a Friday night.

Above: **A group of young singers and a musician in downtown Reykjavík.**

Opposite: **Many Icelanders learn to play chess at an early age.**

In the bars and dance halls, young people drink, talk, dance, meet friends, argue, dance more, and talk more. The party generally goes on until around 5 or 6 A.M. Most teenagers go to the bars with groups of friends, while those in their 20s are more likely to be in couples.

Despite the liberated nature of women, it is more common for boys to ask girls out on dates than vice versa. The same is not necessarily true of invitations to dance. Indeed, unwary visiting foreigners may be surprised at the amount of attention paid to them by uninhibited young people, happy to strike up a conversation with a stranger or to invite them to join in the dancing.

FESTIVALS

THE LONG DARK DAYS of winter are enlivened by a number of festivals which help cheer the spirits of Icelanders during the bad weather. In summertime, festivals take advantage of the extended daylight.

NEW YEAR'S EVE

New Year's Eve is celebrated in Reykjavík with a vast and spectacular fireworks display at midnight. Many communities celebrate with gatherings around large bonfires.

Above: **Festivities associated with Independence Day celebrations, with Icelanders dressing up in traditional costumes.**

Opposite: **The traditional New Year's Eve fireworks display in Reykjavík.**

CALENDAR OF FESTIVALS

Date	Festival
January 1	New Year's Day
Late January (first sighting of sun)	Sun Coffee
January/February (varies)	Thorrablót
March (seven weeks before Easter)	Bolludagur, Sprengidagur, Öskudagur
April (varies)	Easter
Third Thursday in April	first day of summer
First Sunday in May	Seamen's Day
June 17	Independence Day
First weekend of August	Verslunarmannahelgi
September	Réttir
December 25	Christmas

Many families take a walk downtown in December to see the dazzling lights on Christmas trees.

THE CHRISTMAS SEASON

In Iceland, Christmas is a serious day for religious celebration and for spending time with the family. Christmas festivities peak on Christmas Eve. This is the day when Icelanders exchange presents and eat the traditional Christmas dinner. The main course is *hangikjöt* (HANG-i-KYOHT), a traditional form of smoked lamb, with boiled potatoes and green beans. This is preceded by a large bowl of rice pudding into which a single almond has been mixed. Whoever gets the portion with the almond receives a special present. The day before Christmas Eve also has its traditional meal, featuring the skate fish.

Christmas Eve is preceded by 13 days that are each marked by the arrival of a different Father Christmas. These 13 Father Christmases are the children of Gryla, a mean troll woman who likes to eat naughty children. Icelandic mothers evoke the threat of Gryla to encourage their children to be good. Gryla's sons are benign but mischievous, as is suggested by their names, such as Candle-Beggar, Bowl-Licker, and

Door-Slammer. One Icelandic ritual for these 13 nights before Christmas is for children to leave a shoe by the window. The shoe will then be filled by a gift from that day's Father Christmas.

The Christmas season extends for 13 days after Christmas as the Father Christmases leave one at a time.

SUN COFFEE

Communities surrounded by mountains, such as Ísafjördur in the western fjords, lose all sight of the sun for an extended time in winter, even on days that are not overcast. In such communities, there is a celebration of the first day on which the sun becomes visible over the surrounding mountains at a festival called Sun Coffee. People celebrate the first sighting of the sun with a special serving of coffee and fancy cakes.

Icelanders celebrating Sun Coffee at a buffet in Reykjavík.

THORRABLÓT

Thorrablót is a welcoming of the traditional month of Thorra, which begins midwinter in January or February. Days are still very dark at this time, so this festival provides a welcome opportunity to party. Traditional food is eaten on this day. One of the most traditional dishes is *hákarl* (HAO-kahl), shark meat that has been softened by leaving it to rot for three to six months. It is washed down with *brennivín* (BREN-i-vin), an Icelandic form of vodka made from distilled potatoes flavored with angelica. This firewater has the nickname "black death," due to its strong alcoholic kick. This seems handy for making the rotten shark meat more palatable.

Icelanders helping themselves to the traditional foods of *hákarl* and *svid* on Thorrablót.

Another traditional food to be eaten on Thorrablót is *svid* (SVEETH). This is a dish that makes full use of the sheep that are such an important part of Icelandic farming. *Svid* is the head of a sheep, singed to remove the wool, then boiled. It is served complete with the tongue and eyes! Again, appropriately enough, it is washed down with *brennivín*.

BEGINNING OF LENT

Ash Wednesday and the two days before it are enjoyable celebrations for Icelandic children. Monday is *Bolludagur* (BOH-tloo-DAH-gor), named after the *bollur* (BOH-tlor) that mothers bake for this day. These are tasty eclairs filled with cream and covered in chocolate. By tradition, children are given a little flail on this day. It is their holiday task to catch their

parents unguarded so that they can whip them on the rump with the flail. For each successful attack a child receives one of the delicious *bollur*.

The next day, Shrove Tuesday, is *Sprengidagur* (SPREN-gi-DAH-gor). This is a day of feasting on the traditional meal of *saltkjöt* (SALT-kioht)—salted mutton—with mashed potatoes and green beans.

The next day is Ash Wednesday, *Öskudagur* (EHSK-oo-DAH-gor). On this day, children make little pouches with fabric and run after unsuspecting grown-ups, trying to surreptitiously attach as many pouches as possible to their backs. In the past, these pouches would have been full of ashes. These days, children also dress up in costumes and go trick-or-treating to gather candies, similar to Halloween in the United States.

EASTER

Easter is celebrated with Easter eggs and perhaps a trip to church, much as in the United States. It is the center of a lengthy break in the school calendar. Families often go to their country houses at this time.

Icelanders claiming their seats to get a good view of the Independence Day parade.

OTHER FESTIVALS

FIRST DAY OF SUMMER The first day of summer is celebrated on the third Thursday in April. There are parades on this day and candy for the children. Despite the purpose of the day, it often rains.

SEAMEN'S DAY Icelanders celebrate their traditional link with the sea on the first Sunday in June. This festival celebrates the fishermen and other workers of the sea, who make such an important contribution to the Icelandic economy. There are parades in communities close to the sea, while ships hold an open day in port so that landlubbers can get a taste of life on the ocean.

INDEPENDENCE DAY June 17 is the day of a big parade in celebration of the declaration of independence in 1944. On this day there is street theater and music in Reykjavík and daylong festivities in a carnival

atmosphere. Everybody turns up to watch the parade and takes part in the festivities.

VERSLUNARMANNAHELGI Also known as businessperson's weekend, this is a long weekend break on the first weekend in August. On this occasion, Icelanders traditionally take to the countryside and go camping.

Besides camping, young people gather for their own weekend festivals, which take advantage of the long days of light. Bands perform nonstop, while Icelandic youths party and avoid sleeping until they collapse in exhaustion.

RÉTTIR In September in rural areas, it is necessary to gather the sheep, which have roamed freely during the summer. They are rounded up into large sheep pens so that they can be sorted and claimed by their owners, who maintain them through the winter. This gathering is also the occasion for a rural festival, with dancing, eating, and drinking going on in the evenings.

FOOD

THE DIET OF ICELANDERS is a healthy one as is evident in the longevity of the people. This is probably related to the large part fish plays in Icelandic meals. It is not, however, a strikingly tasty diet. Few spices or herbs are used to add flavor to most Icelandic cooking. Indeed, "bland" might best describe most typical Icelandic foods, with the exception of certain barely-palatable traditional food.

Icelanders characteristically breakfast on a pancake or cereal with fruit juice and coffee. Lunch might be an open sandwich or a buffet of cold cuts, also known as a smorgasbord. Afternoon coffee is often accompanied by cake. The main meal of the day, which may be hot or cold, is eaten in the evening and is likely to involve either fish or lamb. Dairy products are popular for dessert.

Left: **Fast foods such as hot dogs and hamburgers are becoming more and more popular with the young.**

Opposite: **A popular Icelandic dessert is *skyr* (SKOOR). This is a yogurt-like dairy product, made from milk curd. On its own it is low in fat and high in calcium. It is often eaten with cream or mixed with fruit or sugar, which may be less healthy but is certainly delicious. During berry season, the various wild berries of Iceland make a popular dessert with cream.**

A different preparation of lamb particularly suited for lunchtime is *kæfa* (KAY-vah), a paté made from lamb liver. It goes well on dark rye bread.

REGULAR DISHES

Fish is the mainstay of Icelandic cooking. A typical Icelandic dinner is boiled cod or haddock with boiled potatoes and green beans, plus a butter sauce. Other fish staples include salmon, herring, perch, sole, plaice, or halibut.

Fish finds a place at the lunch table, too, either smoked or pickled to be eaten on rye bread. Dried fish also serves as a snack or portable meal. Dehydrated haddock fillets are sold throughout Iceland and are surprisingly tasty. One tears off a strip with the teeth and then chews thoroughly. Alternatively, a strip of dried fish can be eaten with butter. The fish tastes quite delicate with a slightly salty edge and makes for a satisfying snack or light meal.

The other staple of Icelandic meals is lamb or mutton. *Hangikjöt*, literally hung-lamb, is lamb that has been hung to be smoke-cured. It is a traditional element of the Christmas meal but is also popular at other times. It might be served with boiled potatoes and pickled cabbage. *Saltkjöt* (SALT-kyoht) is salt-mutton, another way of preserving lamb. It might be served with mashed potatoes and green beans.

Vegetables are not particularly common or cooked in particularly imaginative ways. Some vegetables and fruit are locally produced in greenhouses heated by geothermal energy. Otherwise, all vegetables are imported, which makes them expensive and not especially fresh.

Both lunch and dinner often feature Icelandic rye bread, which comes in many different forms. There is also a form of rye pancake that is popular.

TRADITIONAL FOODS

Many of Iceland's traditional foods seem extravagant or even distasteful to the modern generation as well as to foreigners. Many of the most distinctive dishes retain an association with specific holidays, particularly Thorrablót.

Some of the most alarming-sounding traditional dishes involve making full use of every part of a slaughtered sheep. Offal from a sheep is minced together with its blood and served in the sheep's stomach to make *slátur* (SLAO-tor). Another delicacy that takes some getting used to makes use of pickled ram's testicles.

Enjoying some shark meat.

Whale meat is traditionally cured by hanging strips of blubber under a bridge for months until they turn black, at which point they can be eaten. *Hákarl* is shark meat that has been matured by burying it for three to six months to allow it to putrefy. The rotted shark meat then smells terribly ripe. It is eaten raw in small chunks washed down with *brennivín* at Thorrablót.

Another local delicacy is puffin. These pretty little birds are caught in nets, especially on the Westmann Islands, as a source of food. They can be broiled and taste something like calf's liver.

FAST FOODS

Fast foods such as hot dogs and hamburgers are steadily rising in popularity in Iceland. It is no longer unusual to find an Icelander eating a hot dog with a cola drink in hand. Icelanders are avid consumers of Coca Cola.

In fact, Iceland has one of the highest consumption of Coca Cola per capita in the world! In Reykjavík, there are numerous fast food outlets. Currently, there are three McDonalds and just as many KFCs (Kentucky Fried Chicken). The convenience of fast foods is a relief for some Icelanders who work long hours and have no time to cook. Microwave dinners are also fast gaining popularity.

COFFEE

Coffee is drunk very widely throughout Iceland. It is practically the only beverage that is readily available throughout Iceland at low cost. Icelanders drink coffee at breakfast, after meals, and with a light snack or cake in midafternoon.

ALCOHOLIC DRINKS

Iceland, like the United States, opted for prohibition of all alcoholic beverages in the early part of the 20th century. In Iceland, the move satisfied a Lutheran temperance lobby and made a political statement, since the revenue from tax on alcohol went to Denmark. Wine was legalized in 1921, and in 1935 a national referendum voted to legalize spirits. Beer, however, remained illegal until 1989.

The ban on beer was finally lifted because it had become moot. The original reasoning argued that if young people could not drink beer, they would not be attracted by stronger drinks, which in any case would be too expensive for them. In the absence of beer, they would stay untainted by alcohol. Such reasoning was thoroughly disproved by the traditions of Friday night in Reykjavík. Indeed, some bars discovered a loophole that allowed them to add a shot of spirits to a glass of nonalcoholic beer, which made a beverage as alcoholic as beer (but worse-tasting).

Another anomaly of the old system was that Icelanders arriving from abroad were allowed to import a quota of beer. The result was that on the arrival of every flight, Icelanders stopped at the duty free shop to buy their legal crate of imported beer and then carried their luggage and beverages back to Reykjavík.

On March 1, 1989, known as Beer Day, a vote in the Althing made alcoholic beer once again legal in Iceland. An Icelandic brewing company now brews its own beer as well as foreign beers under license. The cost of beer is strikingly high compared with other countries. This, however, does not seem to discourage its consumption, particularly on the weekends in Reykjavík.

Iceland's distinctive spirit is *brennivín*, "burning-wine." This is a type of vodka made from distilled potatoes and flavored with angelica. Its nickname is "black death," which suggests the perils of drinking too

Drinking coffee is almost a national pastime in Iceland.

Getting greenhouse-grown red bell peppers ready for the supermarket.

much of this strong spirit. *Brennivín* features in the traditional feasting of Thorrablót. It is also considered an antidote to the cold bleak weather, particularly in the interior. Thus, coffee spiked with *brennivín* is called "mountain coffee," the kind of coffee that keeps the farmers who have to work in the mountains warm on chilly days.

KITCHENS AND MARKETS

Icelandic kitchens, like Icelandic homes in general, tend to be very up-to-date and well-equipped. Microwave ovens are commonplace. Kitchens are kept very clean.

Foodstuffs are bought by Icelanders in supermarkets, which are just like small supermarkets in the United States or Europe, but much more expensive. The only exceptions to the high cost of food are certain local products, most notably caviar and dried fish, which are both quite cheap. There is a far greater variety of fish in most Icelandic supermarkets than in Europe or the United States. Considerable care is taken to keep the fish, which is usually quite a recent catch, as fresh as possible.

Feasting is an important part of many festivals. Extended families gather for such traditional meals as Christmas and Easter. The festival of Thorrablót calls for the inclusion of both family and friends in the celebration.

EATING OUT

Dining out is not much of a tradition for Icelanders although there are quite a few fast food restaurants around. Reykjavík has a range of international restaurants, although strongly spiced or hot dishes are generally toned down to satisfy local tastes.

There are numerous street kiosks throughout Reykjavík for picking up a quick snack on the go. These serve up French fries, pizza, sausages, and soft drinks, all relatively cheaply. It is also possible to get an economical plate of fish and chips.

There is much more of a traditional café and bar scene. It is easy to get light meals in Reykjavík's cafés. Such meals include open-topped sandwiches, stuffed pancake dishes, or a smorgasbord, as well as pastries, cakes, and coffee. These cafés are generally pleasant places for sitting around. Bars also serve light meals. Indeed, many cafés by day are bars by night.

On the whole, restaurants tend to be upmarket and suitable for special occasions. Icelanders often dress up to go to a restaurant, where it is difficult to pay less than $30 for a meal, even without drinks, and easy to pay substantially more.

STEIKTAR HEILAGFISKI (BAKED HALIBUT)

1 slice halibut (can also be substituted with cod or hake), $1\frac{1}{2}$ to 2 inches thick
3 tablespoons melted butter
1 teaspoon salt
$\frac{1}{4}$ teaspoon pepper
1 cup canned tomatoes
$\frac{1}{2}$ teaspoon sugar
1 medium onion
$\frac{1}{2}$ cup heavy cream

Rinse the halibut and pat dry with a kitchen cloth or paper towel. Remove the skin carefully. Grease the baking dish with some of the butter. Season the halibut with salt and pepper then place it in the baking dish. Brush the halibut with the remaining melted butter. Mash the canned tomatoes and add sugar to it. Then pour the mixture over the fish. Cut the medium-sized onion into thin slices and place it over the fish. Bake the fish in a hot oven at 400°F (200°C). After 20 minutes, take the dish out and pour cream over the fish. Bake the fish for another 10 minutes before it is ready to be served.

HRISGRJONAABAETIR (RICE DESSERT WITH FRUIT OR BERRY JAM)

1⅓ cup milk
¼ cup rice
¼ teaspoon salt
1 tablespoon butter
¼ cup sugar
1 teaspoon blanched, chopped almonds
2 tablespoons sugar
⅔ cup whipping cream (or up to 1 cup)
¼ cup berry jam or fruit

Heat the milk in a pan. Wash the rice and add it to the milk. Cook the rice until it becomes soft. The rice will take approximately half an hour to cook. Once cooked, add salt, butter, ¼ cup sugar and the blanched, chopped almonds. Let the mixture cool. Meanwhile, whip the cream until it becomes stiff and add 2 tablespoons of sugar. Fold the whipped cream into the rice mixture. Serve in a glass bowl. Press the center of the rice dessert down gently and fill the depression with fruit or berry jam.

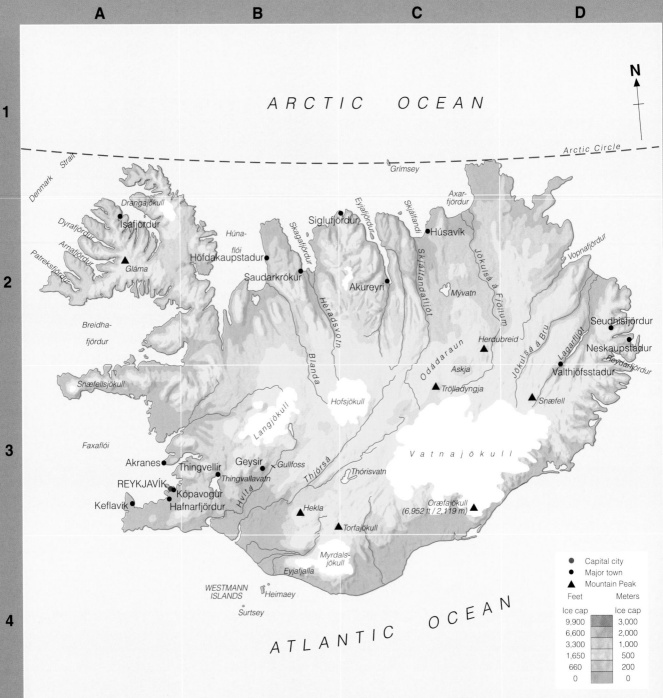

MAP OF ICELAND

Akranes, A3
Akureyri, C2
Arctic Ocean, B1
Arnafjördur, A2
Askja, C3
Atlantic Ocean, B4
Axarfjördur, C1

Blanda River, B2
Breidhafjördur, A2

Denmark Strait, A1
Drangajökull, A1
Dyrafjördur, A2

Eyjafjalla, B4
Eyjafjördur, C1

Faxaflói, A3

Geysir, B3
Gláma, A2
Grímsey, C1
Gullfoss, B3

Hafnarfjördur, A3
Heimaey, B4

Hekla, B3
Héradsvotn, B2
Herdubried, C2
Höfdakaupstadur, B2
Hofsjökull, B3
Húnaflói, B2
Húsavík, C2
Hvítá, B3

Isafjördur, A2

Jökulsá á Bru, D3
Jökulsá á Fjöllum, C2

Keflavík, A3
Kópavogur, A3

Lagarfljót, D2
Langjökull, B3

Myrdalsjökull, B4
Myvatn, C2

Neskaupstadur, D2

Odádaraun, C3
Oraefajökull, C3

Patreksfjördur, A2

Reydarfjördur, D2
Reykjavík, A3

Saudarkrókur, B2
Siglufjördur, C2
Skagafjördur, B2
Skjálfandafljót, C2
Skjálfandi, C1
Snaefell, D3
Snaefellsjökull, A3

Suedhisfjördur, D2
Surtsey, B4

Thingvallavatn, B3
Thingvellir, B3
Thjórsá, B3
Thórisvatn, C3
Torfajökull, C3
Trölladyngja, C3

Valthjöfsstadur, D3
Vatnajökull, C3
Vopnafjördur, D2

Westmann Islands, B4

ECONOMIC ICELAND

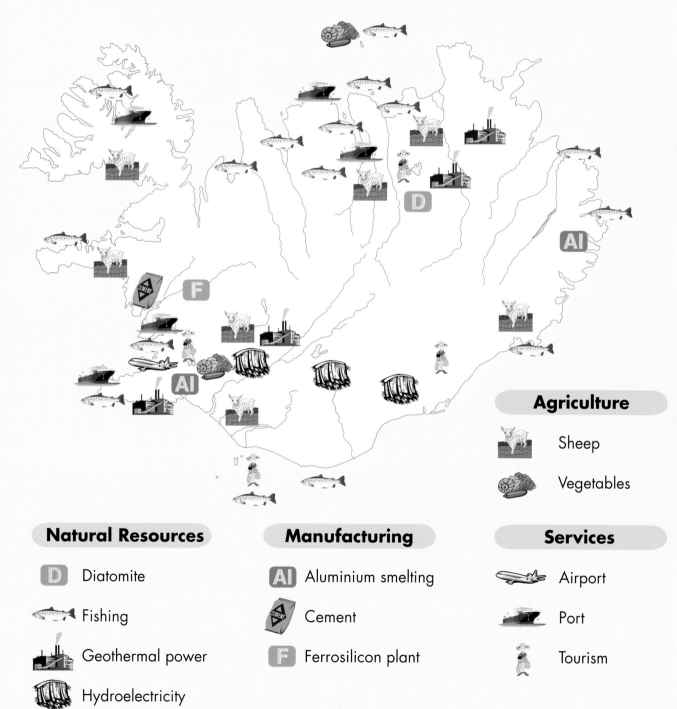

Agriculture

Sheep

Vegetables

Natural Resources

D Diatomite

Fishing

Geothermal power

Hydroelectricity

Manufacturing

Al Aluminium smelting

Cement

F Ferrosilicon plant

Services

Airport

Port

Tourism

ABOUT
THE ECONOMY

OVERVIEW

Iceland's economy has changed from being highly regulated to a free-market capitalistic one. Although still heavily dependent on fishing and the fish manufacturing industry, Iceland has diversified its economy into manufacturing (software production and biotechnology among others) and the service-oriented industry. Tourism is booming in Iceland where it has found a market niche for ecotourism and whale watching. Iceland's healthy economy helps its people enjoy a low unemployment rate and a high standard of living.

GROSS DOMESTIC PRODUCT

$13.05 billion (2005 estimate)

LAND USE

Arable land 0.07 percent, others 99.93 percent (2005 estimates)

NATURAL RESOURCES

Fish, hydropower, geothermal power, diatomite

CURRENCY

1 Icelandic krona (Ikr) = 100 aurar
Notes: 5,000; 2,000; 1,000; 500 krona
Coins: 100, 50, 10, 5, 1 aurar
1 USD = 69.73 ISK (August 2006)

INFLATION RATE

4.5 percent (2005 estimate)

AGRICULTURAL PRODUCTS

Potatoes, vegetables, mutton, dairy products, fish

INDUSTRIES

Fish processing, aluminum smelting, ferrosilicon production, geothermal power, tourism

MAJOR EXPORTS

Marine products 60.5 percent, agricultural products 2.1 percent, manufacturing products 35.1 percent, others 2.3 percent (2005 estimates)

MAJOR IMPORTS

Food and beverages 9 percent, industrial supplies 26 percent, fuels and lubricants 9 percent, capital goods (except transport equipment) 22 percent, transport equipment 16 percent, consumer goods 18 percent (2005 estimates)

EXPORT PARTNERS

United Kingdom, Germany, Netherlands, United States, Spain, Denmark, France

IMPORT PARTNERS

Germany, United States, Norway, Denmark, United Kingdom, Sweden, Netherlands

WORKFORCE

165,900 (2005 estimate)

UNEMPLOYMENT RATE

2.1 percent (2005 estimate)

CULTURAL ICELAND

Ólafsvík
Regular sightings of blue, minke, and humpback whales can be made in this popular whale watching center.

Jökulsárgljúfur National Park
A pleasant hike around this park will take visitors to a horseshoe shaped canyon and to Dettifoss, Europe's most powerful waterfall.

Húsavík
This is one of Iceland's popular spots for whale watching. Porpoises and dolphins are also sighted here.

Lake Myvatn
Numerous picturesque volcanoes and hot springs can be found here. It is also home to an amazing collection of nesting birds.

Reykjavik
Iceland's capital is rich in cultural attractions and exciting nightlife. The Reykjavik Arts Festival, Cultural Night, and Jazz Festival are just some of the cultural treats here.

Blue Lagoon
Bathing in this mineral-rich, geothermally heated pool is said to be excellent for curing skin problems.

Thingvellir
Home to the first Icelandic parliament, the Althing.

Heimaey Island
At the Hæna, Kafhellir, and Hani cliffs reside the world's largest puffin colonies. Watch puffin chicks take flight from these cliffs every August.

Geysir
Great Geyser used to spout regularly to a height of 200 feet (60 m) but is now rather quiet. Strokkur, which is nearby, erupts every few minutes to a height of up to 100 feet (30 m).

Gullfoss
This spectacular waterfall is formed where the Hvítá River tumbles 105 feet (32 m) into a 1.5 mile (2.4 km) ravine.

ABOUT
THE CULTURE

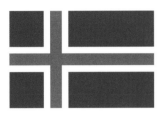

OFFICIAL NAME
Republic of Iceland (Lydhveldidh Island)

FLAG DESCRIPTION
Blue with a red cross outlined in white extending to the edges of the flag; the vertical part of the cross is shifted to the hoist side in the style of the Dannebrog (Danish flag)

TOTAL AREA
Total: 39,768 square miles (103,000 sq km)
Land: (100,250 sq km); Water: (2,757 sq km)

CAPITAL
Reykjavík

ETHNIC GROUPS
Mixture of descendants of Norse and Celts 94 percent, population of foreign origin 6 percent

RELIGIOUS GROUPS
Lutheran Church of Iceland 85.5 percent, Reykjavik Free Church 2.1 percent, Roman Catholic Church 2 percent, Hafnarfjordur Free Church 1.5 percent, other Christian 2.7 percent, others 3.8 percent, unaffiliated 2.4 percent

BIRTH RATE
13.73 births per 1,000 Icelanders (2005 estimate)

DEATH RATE
6.68 deaths per 1,000 Icelanders (2005 estimate)

AGE STRUCTURE
0–14 years: 22.1 percent
15–64 years: 66.2 percent
65 years and over: 11.7 percent (2005 estimates)

MAIN LANGUAGES
Icelandic, English, Danish

LITERACY RATE
People ages 15 and above who can read and write: 99.9 percent (2005 estimate)

NATIONAL HOLIDAYS
New Year's Day (January 1), Maundy Thursday (on the Thursday before Easter), Good Friday (on the Friday before Easter), Easter Sunday, Easter Monday, First Day of Summer (third or fourth Thursday in April), May Day (May 1), Ascension Day (sixth Thursday after Easter), Whit Sunday (eighth Monday after Easter), Independence Day (June 17), Commerce Day (first Monday of August), Christmas Day (December 25), Boxing Day (December 26)

LEADERS IN POLITICS
Ólafur Ragnar Grímsson—president since 1996
Halldór Ásgrímsson—prime minister since 2004
Sveinn Björnsson—first president of independent Iceland (1944–52)

TIME LINE

IN ICELAND	IN THE WORLD

325 B.C.
Discovery of "Thule," believed to be Iceland.

323 B.C.
Alexander the Great's empire stretches from Greece to India.

A.D. 600
Height of Mayan civilization.

A.D. 700
Irish monks and Norse settlers arrive in Iceland.

874
Ingólfur Arnarson "The First Settler" builds his home near Reykjavík. More settlers come from Scandinavia in this "Age of Settlement."

930
End of "Age of Settlement." The Icelandic parliament, the Althing, is founded.

1000
Christianity is adopted as Iceland's official religion.

1000
The Chinese perfect gunpowder and begin to use it in warfare.

1100
Rise of the Incan Civilization in Peru.

1120–1300
The Saga Age: old sagas or tales are written down.

1206–1368
Genghis Khan unifies the Mongols and starts conquest of the world. At its height, the Mongol Empire under Kublai Khan stretches from China to Persia and parts of Europe and Russia.

1220–62
The Sturlunga Age: a period of anarchy

1262
Iceland is ruled by the king of Norway.

1380
Iceland and Norway enter a union with Denmark.

1558–1603
Reign of Elizabeth I of England

1776
U.S. Declaration of Independence

1789–99
The French Revolution

1800
The Danish king abolished the Althing; Icelanders begin to seek independence.

1800
The start of the Industrial Age

1843
Independence movement brings about reinstatement of the Althing.

1861
The U.S. Civil War begins.

IN ICELAND	IN THE WORLD
	1869 The Suez Canal is opened.
1904 Iceland is granted home rule.	
	1914 World War I begins.
1915 Iceland gets its own flag.	
	1939 World War II begins.
1940 British troops occupy Iceland to defend the country against German invasion.	
1941 The United States takes over to protect Iceland.	**1941** Japan attacks Pearl Harbor.
1944 Iceland becomes an independent republic on June 17th.	**1945** The United States drops atomic bombs on Hiroshima and Nagasaki.
1949 Iceland becomes a founding member of NATO.	**1949** The North Atlantic Treaty Organization (NATO) is formed.
1951 The United States builds the Keflavík airbase.	**1957** The Russians launch Sputnik.
1976 A 200-mile fishing limit off the coast of Iceland is agreed.	**1966–69** The Chinese Cultural Revolution.
1980 Vigdís Finnbogadóttir is the first woman in the world democratically elected as head of state.	
1986 Presidents Gorbachev and Reagan meet at Reykjavík to discuss ending the Cold War.	**1986** Nuclear power disaster at Chernobyl in Ukraine
1994 Iceland enters the European Economic Area.	**1991** Breakup of the Soviet Union.
2000 Reykjavík is voted the European City of Culture for the millennium.	**1997** Hong Kong is returned to China.
	2001 Terrorists crash planes in New York, Washington D.C., and Pennsylvania.
2004 Prime Minister David Oddson steps down after serving for 13 years.	**2003** War in Iraq begins.

GLOSSARY

Althing
The Icelandic parliament, founded in A.D. 930 and still functioning.

berserkir (BAIR-zerh-kahr)
Medieval warriors who dedicated themselves to Odin.

brennivín (BREN-i-vin)
A type of vodka made from distilled potatoes and flavored with angelica.

geyser
A hot-water spring that builds up pressure so that it shoots a jet of water high into the air.

glíma (GLEE-mah)
A traditional form of wrestling in which wrestlers wear harnesses on their thighs and hips which their opponent grabs in an attempt to throw them to the ground.

godi; pl. **godar** (GO-thi; GO-thar)
The chieftains of medieval Iceland.

hangikjöt (HANG-i-YOHT)
Literally hung-lamb; a dish made of lamb that has been hung to be smoke-cured.

hákarl (HAO-kahl)
Shark meat that has been matured by burying it for three to six months to allow it to putrefy. It is eaten raw in small chunks.

kæfa (KAY-vah)
A pâté made from lamb liver.

patronymic
The system of identifying someone by using their father's name followed by the Icelandic term for -son or -daughter.

Ragnarok
Doom of the gods; the final battle when the gods of Norse pagan tradition will lose to the forces that oppose them.

saltkjöt (SALT-kyoht)
Salt-mutton; a way of preserving lamb.

sandur (SAND-or)
Wastelands of black sand and volcanic debris deposited by run-off flowing from glaciers.

skalds (SKAHLDS)
The poets who recited Old Icelandic poetry.

skyr (SKOOR)
A yogurt-like dairy product made from milk curd.

slátur (SLAO-tor)
Offal from a sheep minced together with its blood and served in the sheep's stomach.

solfataras
Areas of hot ground that are associated with volcanic activity.

thing (thing)
A local parliament and meeting place in the Middle Ages.

FURTHER INFORMATION

BOOKS

Anderson, Robert. *The Ghosts of Iceland*. Belmont, CA: Wadsworth Publishing, 2004.

Byock, Jesse L. *Viking Age Iceland*. London: Penguin (Non-Classics), 2001.

Gudmundsson, Einar Már. *Angels of the Universe*. London: Mare's Press, 1995.

Janoda, Jeff. *Saga: A Novel of Medieval Iceland*. Chicago, IL: Academy Chicago Publishers, 2005.

Karlsson, Gunnar. *The History of Iceland*. Minneapolis, MN: University of Minnesota Press, 2000.

Laxness, Halldór. *Independent People*. London: Harvell Press, 1999.

Thordarson, Thor and Armann Hoskuldsson. *Classical Geology in Europe 3: Iceland*. Hertfordshire, UK: Terra Publishing, 2002.

WEB SITES

A Gateway to Iceland. www.iceland.is

Central Intelligence Agency World Factbook (select Iceland from country list). www.cia.gov/cia/publications/factbook/index.html

Iceland Review Online. www.icelandreview.com

Lonely Planet World Guide: Iceland. www.lonelyplanet.com/destinations/europe/iceland

Your Official Guide to Iceland. www.icetourist.is

FILMS

Children of Nature. Icelandic Film Corporation, 1991.

Europe. Goldhill Video, 1998.

Iceland and Greenland. Pilot Film and TV Productions Ltd, 2004.

Trekking in Iceland. New Media, 1995.

MUSIC

Björk. *Post*. Elektra/ Wea, 1995.

Sigur Rós. *Tak*. Geffen Records, 2005.

Songs and Dances from Iceland. Arc Music, 1994.

BIBLIOGRAPHY

Ban, W. Bryant, Jr., and Gudmundur Erlingsson, translators. *Six Old Icelandic Tales*. Lanham, MD: University Press of America, 1993.

Durrenberger, E. Paul and Gísli Pálsson. *The Anthropology of Iceland*. Iowa City, IA: University of Iowa Press, 1989.

Hastrup, Kirsten. *Island of Anthropology: Studies in Past and Present Iceland*. Philadelphia, PA: Coronet Books, 1990.

Lacy, Terry G. *Ring of Seasons: Iceland—Its Culture and History*. Ann Arbor: The University of Michigan Press, 1998.

Lerner Publications. *Iceland—In Pictures*. Minneapolis, MN: Department of Geography, Lerner Publications, 1991.

Roberts, David and Jon Krakauer. *Iceland: Land of the Sagas*. New York: H.N. Abrams, 1990.

Russell, William. *Iceland*. Vero Beach, FL: The Rourke Book Co., Inc., 1994.

Icelandic Nature Conservation Association. www.inca.is

Ministry for Foreign Affairs. www.mfa.is

Statistics Iceland. www.statice.is

United Nations. www.un.org

INDEX